Gandhian Approach to Peace

About the Author

Dr. Monika Spolia is born in Punjab (India) and grew up in Canada. She finished. her BSc. in Physics and Mathematics at the University of British Columbia, Canada. Always fascinated by cultures and grass-root movements, she travelled to India to pursue her Masters in Anthropology at the University of Rajasthan, Jaipur. During this time, she also conducted independent research on Adivasi (indigenous people) in India and worked on a resettlement action plan for villages in Rajasthan. She completed her Doctorate in Anthropology and Political Science.

She is the Chief Editor and founder publisher of *Bharat Times* Newspaper in Montreal, Canada since its inception in 2003. Her research articles on Global Similarities in Music and Dance and on Adivasis have appeared in Anthropology related books.

In recognition of her achievements, she received the Outstanding Business Person Award 2005, from NACOI, National Association of Canadians of Origins in India, at 25th Banquet Award Ceremony in Montreal, Canada.

In 2006, she was the 'Hind Ratan' Award nominee (Indian Jewel Award) from NRI Welfare Society of India for the year 2006 in regards to the achievements in mass-media communication and implementation of a full-fledged intercultural newspaper in Canada.

Gandhian Approach to Peace

Dr. Monika Spolia

CONCEPT PUBLISHING COMPANY PVT. LTD.
NEW DELHI-110059

ISBN-13 : 978-81-8069-963-4

First Published 2013

Published and Printed by

Concept
Since 1974

Concept Publishing Company Pvt. Ltd.
A/15-16, Commercial Block, Mohan Garden
New Delhi-110059 (India)
T: 25351460, 25351794, *F*: 091-11-25357109
E: publishing@conceptpub.com, W: www.conceptpub.com
Editorial Office: H-13, Bali Nagar, New Delhi-110 015, India.

Cataloging in Publication Data--Courtesy: D.K. Agencies (P) Ltd. <docinfo@dkagencies.com>

Spolia, Monika.
Gandhian approach to peace / Monika Spolia.
p. cm.
Includes bibliographical references (p) and index.
ISBN 9788180699634

1. Peace. 2. Nonviolence. 3. Gandhi, Mahatma, 1869-1948. I. Title.

DDC 327.1720954 23

Acknowledgements

I would like to acknowledge my late parents, Om Parkash Spolia and Avinash Spolia, who were the living exemplary Gandhians, guides and my role models. I find a deeper understanding settling in me as I follow in their footsteps.

Vishal Sharma and Gopika Sharma have been by my side in thought and spirit.

I would also like to thank Manes Liautaud for becoming my angel of moral support.

Monika Spolia

Preface

Peace is I.
Peace is in me.
Peace is within me.
Peace lies within *prakriti*.
Peace is the highest moral.
Peace is the utmost principle.
Peace is the foundation of humanity.
In peace is the highest level of education.
Peace lights the *diya* of enlightenment in our hearts.
Peace is the potential in the sea of matter.
Peace is the dynamism of social reality.
Peace is vital life force.
Peace is alive.
Peace is.
Peace.
Peace.
Peace.

In search of peace...
I read books to understand peace.
I watched documentaries to unravel truth.
I volunteered to spread peace.
I joined groups to promote peace.
I travelled to open my mind to peace.
I sought higher education to find answers to peace.

I sought peace in temples.
I sought peace through devotion.
I thought peace is in silence.
I thought peace is in love.
I thought peace is in non-violence.

At last,
I shut my external senses.
I envisioned peace.
Inside me.

Then, I realized
Peace is I.
Peace is in me.
Peace is within me....

Monika Spolia

Contents

1

Introduction

Om Shanti. Om Shanti. Om Shanti

The journey for peace begins as peace is sought for as a denial to violence or non-peace. Then the journey of non-violence as a dynamic praxis begins. Furthermore, peace is realized on the path of the journey of non-violence.

We are surrounded by echoes of 'peace'. We hear the word 'peace' everywhere but hardly anyone realizes what peace is less one knows how to attain it. United Nations has Peace Corps and soldiers are sent in different places to fight for peace. Iraqis are screaming peace as an alternative to war. Soldiers in battlefield with no other alternative but to kill the 'others' have hard time suppressing their outcries of peace. A handful of past-generation conservative-protester hippies are passing on their attractive slogan of 'make love not war'.

Some nations are at war because one of the nations believes that it must bring about peace in the other nation/s by fighting for it. Some religious missionaries are propagating peace by increasing the number of converts in their respective religions. Some schools of thought are trying to reason *via* providing selective knowledge that their ideology is the best for promoting peace. In the name of peace some cults promote conforming in an attempt to multiply their registrations through perhaps rightful propaganda of salvaging the souls.

But where is peace? History has not yet witnessed peace as the aftermath of a war. Number crunching of religious conversions is a state of competition. Selective knowledge is little knowledge which is thought to be more dangerous than not. Conforming is a second hand attempt to duplicate that leads to not being oneself whereas it is the self whose soul needs to be salvaged.

Again where is peace? Before we look for peace it is imperative to establish what it is that we are looking for. What is peace? What does it comprise of? What does it entail? What is the definition of peace?

In ancient times as well as in modern times, in varieties of thoughts and religions, peace has been described in a negative sense (opposed to war) and in a positive sense (social well being and harmony).

Most often peace is mentioned in binary comparison to war. "Peace" in opposition to war is criticized as negative peace by some analysts. On the other hand, "some analysts stress positive peace, defined as social relations marked by considerable equality in life chances, by justice, or even by harmony". Various writers consider peace to exist in social relations among global partners, individuals, groups as well as countries. Some observers ultimately consider peace a stable condition of multi-fold never-ending processes.[1]

Thus, peace must be practised because it is not a theory. Peace revivifies dynamism because it is not static. Peace is a multifold intertwined dimension of human time as it is not linear. Peace is an entire culture and a complete philosophy rather than a mere thought or a concept. Peace is to be sought, felt, contained and shared because it can not simply be given and/or taken. Peace must be invoked inside the soul because it is not to be obtained by asking or demanding. Peace is a loving, harmonious, just and cooperative vital force that must not be described merely as the absence of war phenomenon. Peace is a path that leads to prosperity and well-being. Through the process of peace we must conquer the obstacles that lay in our way of achieving political stability, economic progress, social harmony and ethics, however, not without the caution that "liberty never meant the license to do anything at will."[2]

A Messiah of Peace in most human form, Mahatma Gandhiji had described a simple grassroot praxis of spinning of the wheel not only as a commercial peace but as the economic progress leading to political stability:

> *"I claim for the charkha the honour of being able to solve the problem of economic distress in a most natural, simple, inexpensive and business-like manner. The charkha, therefore, is not only not useless but is a useful and indispensable article for every home. It is the symbol of a nation's prosperity and, therefore, freedom. It is a symbol not of commercial war but of commercial peace."*[3]

The above example of commercial peace is just one of the many folds of the multi-fold never-ending processes of the stable condition of peace brought about by the non-violence philosophy of Gandhiji.

Thus, 'being in peace' is search for 'peace as means' whereas 'peace as an end' only suggests a beginning of the process which when journeyed upon will ultimately lead to peace.

Gandhi Embarks on Journey of Peace

Here is an example of a peaceful journey told by Arun Gandhi, fifth grandson of Mahatma Gandhi as he wrote extensively about Kasturba, wife of Mahatma Gandhi.

This journey will outline the main ethics and principles of Gandhiji as he transformed into 'Mahatma' Gandhi.

Before we reflect on Gandhiji's peaceful journey toward peace, i.e. peace as means and peace as an end, it is imperative and absolutely necessary to find out not only what Gandhiji thought or why Gandhiji thought so; but most importantly 'how Gandhiji thought'. Let's not forget that Gandhiji was a lawyer and at his best, he embarked on a journey to defend the freedom of his home nation. As we see some glimpses of his life, his principles and his reasoning as a lawyer stares at us. To undertake such a huge task as to defend the freedom of one of the world's most populated, aristocratic, spiritual and most diverse nation, one had to believe in it and seek ways to prove it. Gandhiji put that trust in himself to prove that India must be freed.

His methods as a result, such as *ahimsa, satyagraha, sarvodaya,* etc., are the outcome of his barrister work, not in theory but in actual practice in real life.

This journey is not of Gandhiji's alone but Gandhiji as a complete person along with his family, his relatives, his friends, his associates, his colleagues and anybody and everybody with him.

In other words, Gandhiji not only talked about his journey or wrote books on it, or gave speeches on it – he actually lived it. And without a doubt, with complete consent of Kasturba, his wife, his life-long partner.

> Once Gandhi's son, Manilal, at the young age of 12 forgot his reading glasses at home. When Gandhiji found Manilal peering closely at a book, he decided to teach Manilal responsibility by sending him back home, i.e. a five-mile walk, to fetch his glasses. When Manilal reached home and told his mother why, Kasturba sat him down for a quick lunch.
>
> While her son ate, Kasturba sat beside him at the kitchen table. How could she impress upon this 12-year-old boy the importance of his father's strong ideals? How could she make him understand?
>
> "I know how it is to feel that Bapu is demanding too much of you." She paused, studying her son's reaction, then continued. "It happened to me once, on a day long ago. You were only five or six years old, then and we were living in Durban. Remember?"
>
> As Manilal listened in rapt attention, she told him how, in deference to his unorthodox ideas, she had forced herself to empty the chamber pot of one of their Christian houseguests. She spoke of how hurt she had been realizing her husband expected her to degrade herself in this way; how furious she had been, knowing he wanted her to cheerfully defy the teachings of generations of religious leaders. She told how she had lashed back at Mohandas, provoking him to greater anger. Even now, Kasturba said, she could not quite see how an argument about the cleaning of one little chamber pot could be so important as to make him want to drive his wife out of his home in a strange land. Yet that incident, she said, had proved one thing to her, the seriousness of Bapu's beliefs. She had vowed, then and there, that even though she could not, on her own account, accept any of her husband's peculiar new notions unless she was convinced he was right, she would try

> always to understand his way of thinking and, whenever possible acquiesce to his wishes.
>
> "What I do know," Kasturba concluded, "and what you must understand is this: Your father is a good man. He wants you to be a good son, and that is why he asks you to do hard things." Smiling, she ran her fingers through Manilal's unruly hair. "You are a good son, and that is why you must do as he asks – even the hard things. Now finish your lunch quickly and get back to the office before he begins to wonder what has happened to you."
>
> Years later, my father Manilal liked to tell his own children about the day he forgot his spectacles. He would conclude by assuring us that was how he learned not to forget things. But I always sensed that what made him remember the incident so vividly was not his father's stern discipline, but his mother's firm and loving guidance.[4]

Discipline is utmost in the journey of non-violence and for one to live in harmony with other fellow beings, one has to learn to live in harmony with nature itself by abiding to nature's discipline and nature of the discipline. Everyday sun rises, sun sets, moon bestows its brilliance, dawn approaches and sun rises and the cycle continues. In nature, there are cyclical daily periods, weekly periods, monthly periods, etc. Similarly, in the life of a human, the cyclical/periodic discipline follows: periods of age and the corresponding activities. The lesson to learn from above is that to learn stern discipline, loving, however, firm guidance is the simultaneous approach. This in turn displays praxis practise of a theory, or dynamism of a theory of Indian culture, Indian Thought.

> ". . .By 1996 Mohandas K. Gandhi's law practice became the most lucrative in South Africa. . .
>
> Such success brought Mohandas little personal satisfaction. On the contrary, he was feeling as he had earlier in Durban, that he was caught in a meaningless pursuit of material gain, and he feared he was allowing his family to become ensnared also. The Gita's teachings on non-possession and non-attachement, Ruskin's lessons on the dignity of labour, suggested a better way. . .
>
> The obligation to train Kasturba and the boys in self-reliance

> and frugality was weighing heavily upon Mohandas – one reason he wanted his own family, as soon as possible, to become part of the experiment in self-sustaining communal life at Phoenix Settlement. . ."[5]

Embarking on his journey toward peace, Mohandas Karamchand Gandhi drew on the strength of his cross-cultural upbringing, mainly growing up in traditional Indian family and studying abroad based on British education system. As he sought salvation in ancient Indian scriptures, he came across similar patterns of thoughts reflected among 'western' writers as well. One of such writers is John Ruskin, (1819-1900) English critic, essayist, social thinker and reformer, who suggested redistribution of the state wealth as one of the social reforms and emphasized on the dignity of labour that his felt was eventually diminishing with time[6].

In the midst of wanting to help the community, society and humanity in general, Mohandas Karamchand Gandhi adhered not only to stern discipline but also set on a path to take vows which will facilitate his selfless public service. Nevertheless, he never let this falter his responsibility for the welfare of his family — his wife, children, his siblings, etc. In his own very words, Gandhi started his charity at his very home.

Making his wife and children self-sufficient just as much as he, they were to embark on this journey of public service together. And this Mohandas Karamchand Gandhi achieved gradually with communication, role-model of self and education, and definitely not with force or coercion.

> "Sometimes Kasturba, not yet fully comfortable about letting her husband help with housekeeping duties, was startled to see her sons doing "women's work" also – it seemed against the natural order of things. But Mohandas was adamant: Everyone, himself included, must be ready to do anything that needed doing. Since, he had dispensed with all paid help, Kasturba found it difficult to argue with him, in the end, the work got done to her satisfaction. Better yet was seeing the pride Mohandas took in their son's behaviour . . .[7]

Gandhi made some radical changes in the household and Kasturba gave in, however, his logic, i.e. communication, won his reasoning over Kasturba's social conditioning. Most of all, 'in the end, the work got done to Kasturba's satisfaction. The family and family members come to consensus in regards to self-sufficiency. This ended the time of self-indulgence for the family and marked the beginning of an era of selfless public service by the family of Mohandas Karamchand Gandhi.

Gandhi promoted sharing household duties and public duties equally by men and women. He did not mind tending to himself as he also took pride in seeing his son sharing 'women's duties' as well as he encouraged Kasturba to participate and or lead public gathering.

> The problem was that Mohandas, seen by others as a successful attorney, now saw himself only as a failed public servant. His tireless attempts to get South Africa's unjust laws changed – all his editorials, petitions, speeches – had, in his despairing view, achieved almost nothing. The government would not change. . .
>
> . . . He must do more. He must ask more profound questions, make more difficult decisions. . .
>
> Kasturba was not surprised when her husband announced he was taking a vow of poverty for life. She had been expecting some kind of upheaval. She did not protest when he said he actually, they were renouncing all wealth. His explanation reassured her: He had not vowed to earn no money, he said, but simply to keep no money – none, that is, beyond the minimum required for their basic necessities of life. All else would be donated to community service. . .[8]

Mohandas Karamchand Gandhi decided to take his first vow to non-attachment of all material possessions. This did not mean that he disowned himself of any property or money. He had a home, he had all the necessities of a good home, he gave his children good education and values and looked after their welfare till they became on their own. Not for a moment, Gandhi shied away from his family responsibilities or from his willingness to help people.

> . . .Mohandas was instinctively sympathetic towards the Zulus, who had done no harm to the Indians. Nevertheless, his loyalty

> to the British Empire was undiminished; he still believed that, in his words, it "existed for the welfare of the world."..
>
> . . .and Mohandas was acutely aware that many white South Africans still believed that most Indians were slaves, and all were cowards. A correspondent commenting in the Natal Advertiser, for example, on what he viewed as the absurd idea of enlisting Indian soldiers to help fight Zulus, had slyly suggested that "the Indians, so that they may not run away, should be placed in the front line, and then the fight between them and the Natives will be a sight for the gods." How, Mohandas asked himself, could such venomous racial hatred be eradicated? How could such degrading stereotypes be dispelled? Perhaps, he should advise his countrymen to volunteer for combat and ask for frontline duty. Yet, when he contemplated the conflict itself, his only reaction was misery at the thought of so much violence. . .[9]

With the intention of sustaining industrial revolution, colonialism was born with the intention of enslaving in order to create a cheap labour pool and create economic dependence by displacing local population and whereby destabilizing local regional politics and thus stop the growth of existing sustainable development.

This gospel was spread by popularizing negative stereotypes, spreading hatred, and simply and completely placing the 'other', in this case, the colonized on a pedestal of being less savage animal than a human and thereby stripping him of culture, history, rendering him to be dehumanized. *Voillá* ! A puppet ready to be tamed!

As a result, there was so much hatred based on stereotypes! Why? Is it the responsibility of the 'hated' to dispel the myths? Or is it the problem of the 'hater' who lacks education, values, will and reasoning so as not to fall for stereotypes?

Torn between the thought of wanting to fight in order to 'serve' his nation/empire/humanity and feeling miserable at the mere thought of violence, Kasturba came to his rescue and joined him in his 'nursing' mission in Phoenix.

> "I think you should go and help with the wounded," she said. Mohandas was surprised because Kasturba had expressed the thoughts as if she knew what he was about to say. . .

> On June 2, 1906, when the Gandhi family boarded the train at Johannesburg and set out for Phoenix to start a new life, Mohandas felt as if a heavy burden were being lifted from his soul. . .[10]

Here Kasturba is not just agreeing with Gandhi as a 'good' wife should. This is an example of a wife becoming one minded with her husband, an example of two bodies and one soul and mind.

> . . .These Indian Ambulance Corpsmen would spend little more than a month in active service in the field. During that time they would discover, as my grandfather later wrote, "this was no war, but a manhunt.". . .
>
> . . .The doctor, a humane man, told the Indians that he realized their duty as ambulance workers was to carry wounded, not to nurse them, but he was at his wits' end. He had to ask their help, since non-white medical attendants would not touch the Zulus. . ."

At last, Gandhi saw the other side of British Raj. This incidence dispelled the gospel of colonialism being for the welfare of humanity, and rather exposed it bare naked with its intent to hoard cheap labour and create dependency. At this point, he started contemplating his earlier understanding of British Raj being for 'the welfare of the world'.

> . . .white soldiers who had gathered on the other side of the stockade fence to watch the proceedings, were loudly jeering the Indians and cursing the Zulus. Only later did Mohandas realize these were perhaps some of the very soldiers who had inflicted the wounds. . .
>
> Fortunately, there were military men who shared Mohandas' revulsion. As he learned when he got to know some of the soldiers better, these acts committed by troops under the command of a few ruthless and reckless officers did not go unreported. When news of the atrocities became known, the government, to avoid a scandal, simply declared that the "Zulu Rebellion" has been suppressed. The expeditionary force was disbanded. Volunteers, including the Indian Ambulance Corpsmen, were sent home to their wives and families.

> But Mohandas, by then, has made a crucial decision, one that would affect Kasturba as much as himself: He had vowed, for the rest of his life, to observe *brahmacharya*, to practice celibacy. . .[12]

Infliction of misery, racial stigmatization, and endless aimless killings made Gandhi took a vow of celibacy for the rest of his life. Although he realized that this decision is not his alone, it affects one more dear person in his life.

A simple vow of celibacy wasn't that simple at all. He would have to weigh the option of Kasturba's acceptance or rejection of the vow. After all, he married her and vowed to be with her for the rest of his life. His decisions and her decisions must be at consensus level. Gandhi not only pondered on this vow but also discussed it.

> For many years, Mohandas had been pondering the meaning of existence, searching his heart and mind, seeking to understand the purpose of his life. He had brooded about conflicts between his duty to fulfil family responsibilities, and his yearning to serve the larger community. But now, reflecting on the human brutality he had been witnessing and the human misery he was trying to alleviate, a truth he had only dimly perceived was clearly illuminated for him. His conflict was not between competing loyalties or obligations, but between competing values – between the physical and the spiritual.
>
> If spiritual enlightenment was the goal of his striving (and surely it was – he had already given up any claim on the material things of life), there was one more aspect of physical life he must renounce, one more vow he must take. He must now seek that total non-attachment to worldly pleasures, that "desirelessness" which, according to Hindu scriptures, enables men to enjoy freedom of action in this life, and hope for transcendence to a greater existence beyond.
>
> Here is my grandfather's account of his moment of decision, as related in his autobiography, The Story of My Experiments with Truth:
>
> I clearly saw that [as] one aspires to serve humanity with his whole should. . . I should find myself unequal to my task if I were engaged in the pleasures of family life and in the propagation and rearing of children. In a word, I could not

> live both after the flesh and the spirit. . . The prospect of the vow brought a certain kind of exultation, opened out limitless vistas of service. . .[13]

Gandhiji, as a complete person, did not just make decisions on his own. For him, none of his decisions were his alone. Bound by the Vows of marriage, his decision must be shared and approved by his wife, Kasturba.

> I must confess that I had not then fully realized the magnitude and immensity of the task. p.140
>
> Arriving back at Phoenix Settlement, Mohandas had to inform his wife, the woman to whom he had vowed lifelong fidelity, the only other person in the world directly affected by his vow, that he had forsworn sex for life. Just how uneasy he was at the prospect of facing Kasturba is indicated by the fact, disclosed in his autobiography, that he discussed his vow of *brahmacharya* with Chaganlal, Maganlal, and Albert West before even mentioning it to her.
>
> Kasturba's reaction, when he did consult with her, is reported in a single sentence: "She had no objection.". . .[14]

Here again, Kasturba didn't simply consent to her husband's vows. She exemplified it for the rest of her remaining life. Never was there a complain to be had from her, neither she ever held it over Gandhi's head that she had made sacrifices for him. This is because she didn't make any sacrifice for him. She simply in-tuned with the best of her husband and both became one mind.

Well, a simple vow of celibacy was that simple after all because of mutual consent and free-flow communication between husband and wife. Gandhi and Kasturba grew together because Gandhi treated her as equal and he taught, educated and supported her self-sufficiency. Above all, they built this bond of trust between them by being together and growing together. From time to time, they resumed their gender duties, however, they were careful not to be dictated by it and acted out of these duties when applicable and necessary.

> It seems that Ba had decided to serve her guests one of Bapu's

> favourite dishes, the sweet Indian bread known as puranpoli, which must be cooked to order. Each round cake is rolled individually, then wrapped around a sweet stuffing and rolled out again, then roasted and eaten hot off the stove. When Mohandas saw Kasturba preparing the dough and stuffing for the puranpoli, he summoned his sons to the kitchen and conspired with them – in a loud whisper. "Why don't we have a contest with your mother today? Let's see if she can bake cakes as fast as we and our guests can eat them."
>
> "That's a good idea! Let's do it," was Manilal's instant reply. (Like his father – and his son and grandson, I might add – Manilal was an enthusiastic eater.)
>
> Kasturba, of course, had overheard it all. "Well, in that case," she declared amiably, "I challenge you to keep up with me."
>
> The competition began. Kasturba quickly proved her ability to serve perfectly baked cakes to one and all, indefinitely and without pause – or so it seemed. At last, the guests could eat no more. Then Devadas, Ramdas, even Manilal, gave up, but not their father. Mohandas kept eating the puranpoli long after everyone else had finished. He kept eating until all the dough was gone. Ready to claim victory, he confronted Kasturba.
>
> "Won't you give up? Surely you are ready to concede." Then he saw that she was kneading still more dough. He sighed, made a long face, and prepared to start eating again.
>
> "All right. I admit defeat," Kastura smiled sweetly. She was humoring him. "But remember," she added softly, "I am not tired of making puranpoli. Not yet." And with that, both of them burst out laughing.
>
> There is no rejected or resentful or long-suffering wife here, nor is there any troubled, guilt-ridden husband. Instead, I believe this story gives a first glimpse of the new life they were to be exploring together – the affectionate, playful, teasing relationship that those who know Ba and Bapu well in later years have so often recalled.
>
> Whatever, else may have passed between them at this time of crisis in their lives, one thing is clear: Kasturba's willing acceptance of her husband's vows of poverty and celibacy has quieted his private turmoil of mind and spirit. Mohandas now felt free as never before to answer public calls to action. It was not a moment too soon.[15]

We witness Gandhiji's journey toward peace encouraged by his determination, geared by his innate, learned and resulting principles revealed and concluded by search for truth. He tried to reason the endless sufferings and injustices that set him on the path to seek 'truth'. Interestingly, the title 'Mahatma' coincidently befitted him. 'Mahatma' in Hindi means a 'great soul' and refers to a saintly personality who emanates all understanding and wisdom.

Mohandas Karamchand Gandhi rightly achieved the status of a Mahatma because never before a person has been recorded in history who succeeded in abiding by the same ethics and principles which he instilled in his wife and children simply as a way of life; and yet never shied from his worldly responsibilities.

Gandhiji's Ethics and Vows

The necessary ethics and vows on the path to serving humanity are stern discipline, loving and firm guidance, responsibility, education, self-reliance, communication, growing together with one's family and dear ones, and the vows of poverty and celibacy.

As violence begets violence and hate begets hate, discipline begets discipline. If the company one works for is adamant about punctuality, being on time becomes one's habit.

Guidance begets guidance. Simultaneous loving and firm guidance is quite catchy especially when exemplified through one's behaviour as one nurtures children or crosses the path of others.

Responsibility begets responsibility. If a husband/wife acts responsibily considering his/her family, his/her family will also act responsibly.

Education begets education. If one teaches one's children then the trend will trickle down to grandchildren and so on.

Self-reliance begets self-reliance. If the husband is not a burden on his wife and *vice versa*, the family can rise above the everyday biological clock; and the children will follow. This also implies equality of men and women as well as respecting their gender and social roles.

Communication begets communication. If one person talks openly to the other, it opens the communication channels for both to speak freely, seek mutual consent and bond or build rapport.

Growing together begets growing together. Children will tend to follow the family tradition of sharing and caring and learn to do things together for others.

Poverty begets poverty. In this particular case, poverty means not to keep beyond one's comfort zone. If followed in this manner, the wealth will be redistributed among all and not rest in only a few hands amongst many.

Celibacy begets celibacy. In simple terms, this implies fidelity toward one's life partner and avoidance of over indulgence in sex; the rest rests at the mutual consent of the couple.

It is of utmost importance to practise these ethics and principles in one's everyday life so that they can be learnt by others and be passed on. Let's reflect again on the concept of peace as an end and peace as means respectively. Peace as an end is a static moment which is not dynamic, thus, it does not lead to peace. Peace as means is praxis of non-violence which is a vital dynamic process that breathes and lives peace, thus, in the end sustains peace.

When we want peace as an end only, we are unaware of the journey. Being unaware of the journey is all right, however, we have to keep in mind that 'A' begets 'A' and 'B' begets 'B'. So, the question is which approach do we take to cover the journey toward peace? Violence begets violence, so violence is not the right approach. Hate begets hate, so hate is not the right approach. Deception begets deception, so deception is not the right approach. Material gain is a tangible concept and it is not the right approach because peace is intangible, i.e. money does not buy peace. Infidelity starts a vicious circle of lies and deceptions which do not lead to peace. Too much dependency and inequality will lead to more dependency and more inequality that has no sense of peace.

So, it is obvious that we must be very careful in our approach to peace. Moreover, peace has to start with the person who wants peace. The person who wants peace must deploy peaceful means to achieve peace. Deploying peaceful means is the non-violence journey and it is the 'peace as means'.

Deploying peaceful means through the above mentioned ethics and principles, which also deployed by Mahatma Gandhi, lead to peace and harmony with oneself, one's family, one's friends, one's community, one's society, one's nation, world and humanity. And we must deploy mind over matter for this social reform to reflect reality with 'Yes, we can' attitude.

It is necessary to point out that non-violence theory is different from non-violence philosophy. A theory has a specific time line and is contextual whereas a philosophy is applicable anywhere and anytime. Over the course of humankind's history, many great men and women have conducted non-violence approach and have achieved milestones. Nevertheless, Mahatma Gandhi's approach of non-violence has achieved the status of a timeless philosophy because primarily, he experienced non-violence by living it with his family at the grass-root level then he reasoned through, experimented, explored and demonstrated the effect of non-violence philosophy at a national level in India and in South Africa.

Moreover, non-violence philosophy as sought, explored, understood and put in action by Mahatma Gandhi, in its holistic approach details its pragmatism in social fabric of society and in facing challenges of economic upheavals and political instability. Thus, non-violence in praxis is the most plausible path of the journey that leads to peace as means. Since, each mean of peace attainment is an end in itself, non-violence journey is the means that provides peace as the end. Thus, peace must be a non-violent journey.

Notes

1. Borgatta, Edgar F. and Montgomery, Rhonda J. V. (Editors) *Encyclopaedia of Sociology* – 2 (2nd edition). Macmillan Reference USA, New York: 2000. pp. 2044, pa. 2.
2. Attenborough, Richard. (*selected by*) *The Words of Gandhi.* Newmarket Press, New York: 1996. pp. 31, pa. 38.
3. *Ibid.* pp. 31, pa. 2.
4. Gandhi Arun and Sunanda with Yellin, Carol Lynn. *The Forgotten Woman: The Untold Story of Kastur Gandhi, Wife of Mahatma Gandhi.* Zark Mountain Publishers, Arkansas:1998. pp. 121-123.
5. Gandhi Arun and Sunanda with Yellin, Carol Lynn. *The Forgotten Woman: The Untold Story of Kastur Gandhi, Wife of Mahatma Gandhi.* Zark Mountain Publishers, Arkansas:1998. p. 129
6. Ruskin, John. *Mornings in Florence.* (*e-book*) 1886. 182 pages.

7. Gandhi Arun and Sunanda with Yellin, Carol Lynn. *The Forgotten Woman: The Untold Story of Kastur Gandhi, Wife of Mahatma Gandhi*. Zark Mountain Publishers, Arkansas:1998. p. 130
8. Gandhi Arun and Sunanda with Yellin, Carol Lynn. *The Forgotten Woman: The Untold Story of Kastur Gandhi, Wife of Mahatma Gandhi*. Zark Mountain Publishers, Arkansas:1998. p. 131
9. Gandhi Arun and Sunanda with Yellin, Carol Lynn. *The Forgotten Woman: The Untold Story of Kastur Gandhi, Wife of Mahatma Gandhi*. Zark Mountain Publishers, Arkansas:1998. p. 133
10. Gandhi Arun and Sunanda with Yellin, Carol Lynn. *The Forgotten Woman: The Untold Story of Kastur Gandhi, Wife of Mahatma Gandhi*. Zark Mountain Publishers, Arkansas:1998. p. 134-135.
11. Gandhi Arun and Sunanda with Yellin, Carol Lynn. *The Forgotten Woman: The Untold Story of Kastur Gandhi, Wife of Mahatma Gandhi*. Zark Mountain Publishers, Arkansas:1998. p. 137.
12. Gandhi Arun and Sunanda with Yellin, Carol Lynn. *The Forgotten Woman: The Untold Story of Kastur Gandhi, Wife of Mahatma Gandhi*. Zark Mountain Publishers, Arkansas:1998. p. 137-138.
13. Gandhi Arun and Sunanda with Yellin, Carol Lynn. *The Forgotten Woman: The Untold Story of Kastur Gandhi, Wife of Mahatma Gandhi*. Zark Mountain Publishers, Arkansas:1998. p. 139.
14. Gandhi Arun and Sunanda with Yellin, Carol Lynn. *The Forgotten Woman: The Untold Story of Kastur Gandhi, Wife of Mahatma Gandhi*. Zark Mountain Publishers, Arkansas:1998. p. 140.
15. Gandhi Arun and Sunanda with Yellin, Carol Lynn. *The Forgotten Woman: The Untold Story of Kastur Gandhi, Wife of Mahatma Gandhi*. Zark Mountain Publishers, Arkansas:1998. p. 141-142.

2

Concepts Related to Peace

> "Non-Violence is not a garment to be put on and off at will. Its seat is in the heart, and it must be an inseparable part of our being."
> (Mahatma Gandhi quotes Indian philosopher, internationally esteemed for his doctrine of non-violent protest. *(1869-1948).*

The journey for peace begins as peace is sought for as denial to violence or non-peace whereby the journey of non-violence as a dynamic praxis begins. Furthermore, peace is realized on the path of the journey of non-violence. Thus, 'being in peace' is search for 'peace as means' whereas 'peace as an end' only suggests a beginning of the process which followed will ultimately lead to peace. Due to the cyclical nature of the process of 'peace as means' and 'peace as an end', non-violence journey must become a way of life for the person seeking peace. Peace must necessarily be the means to achieve peace as an end.

In a war-torn world with threats of nuclear power, political instability and economic downturn due to mass production of quantity with no quality and inequality in purchasing power and producing in mass quantities, we need to rehash our values and rework our strategies to emerge progressive rather than caving in to support our structures in place.

For us to move forward and progress in long term and short-term, we need to attain balance in quality and quantity. We need to prosper with the ethics and values that will help us co-exist through co-operation. As we seek peace, we will be living peace.

This scope of this study encompasses micro level as well as macro level. In its holistic approach, non-violence philosophy starts at micro-level, i.e. with the individual abiding by principles and ethics, and is gradually applicable at all macro-levels, i.e. nation-wide and world-wide, applying *satyagraha, sarvodaya* (sustainable economic model) and Gandhian anarchy balancing itself into political stability.

Concepts Related to Peace

The concepts detailed below necessarily shed a new light on the unexplained paradigm, as yet, of 'peace must be a non-violent journey'. It is interesting to note that some concepts may be shedding new light, but are ages old common ideas. Some are used indulgently by Indian Anthropologists and are crucial in the understanding of the book and that 'peace must be a non-violent journey'.

Adivasi

Adivasi literally means early inhabitants or original dwellers. *Adivasis* are the indigenous people of India who maintained the early life styles of mankind till the 19th century. There is still a large population of them in India.

Aggression

This phenomenon occurs when violence necessarily infringes on another's rights and freedoms without any reproach or consent or beyond any further negotiations for co-operation and/or co-existence.

Co-existence

Co-existence is the existence of human beings in harmony with each other. In order to attain that level of co-existence, the human beings must also co-exist with nature/elements of nature in harmony. Nature is a living organism since it reproduces and regenerates its elements like, water, vegetation, animal life, etc. Controlling nature's elements does not render its control because one is unaware of the number of its elements. As soon as one element or a phenomenon pertaining to an element is understood, there arise many more yet to be understood. The best knowledge of nature does not come from its man-made controlling mechanisms or machines but by being in-tune with it. Thus, once implemented the phenomenon of co-existence of humans and nature, the phenomenon of co-existence of humans and societies is the natural course to follow – bringing natural order to 'if existing' anarchy.

Co-operation

Co-operation is utmost necessary in order to achieve efficiency and harmony. The task at hand is peace. The fundamental values are humanity. And co-operation is sought at both levels – humans to humans and humans to nature and *vice versa*.

Compromise is the key to cooperation dealt in measures of degrees and extents.

Development

Keeping in mind that mother earth is organic and that energy is a universal constant — i.e. energy can't be created or destroyed; it may only be transferred from one form to another but the total amount of energy never changes (Law of Conservation of Energy) — the development must necessarily be of the sustainable and renewable nature in order to preserve the environment so that these needs can be met not only in the present but also for future generations.

Dharma

The word *dharma* comes from Sanskrit root '*dhri*', meaning to "uphold" or to "sustain", i.e. *dharma* is that which upholds or sustains the positive order of things: the nation, the community, the family and ultimately even the universe.

Religion, duty and righteousness are all included within the concept of *dharma*. Everybody has a *dharma* according to one's place in life. And individuals have different *dharmas* at different times in their lives; therefore, *dharma* is dynamic as well. For example, a child's *dharma* is to respect and obey parents and study; head of the nation's *dharma* is to protect and flourish the country, etc.

Dharma is that minute basic fundamental foothold upon which religion, duty and spirituality stand.

Dharma and its Principles for Gandhiji

Ethics and principles set by Gandhiji are detailed in chapter 1. These are mainly discipline, loving but firm guidance, responsibility, education, self-reliance, communication, growing together with one's family and dear ones, and the vows of poverty and celibacy: this is Gandhiji's *dharma*. See chapter 1 for details.

Earth as an Organism – See Mother Nature/Prakriti

Freedom

Freedom is not freedom when one individual's free act infringes on another's freedom. Gandhiji, giving a comprehensible meaning to it, writes, "My conception of freedom is no narrow conception. It is co-extensive with the freedom of man in all his majesty; and so "Every individual must have the fullest liberty to use his talent consistently with equal use by neighbours, but no one is entitled to the arbitrary use of the gains or, say, the social structure surrounding him. Therefore, he can use his talent not for self only but for the social structure of which he is but a part and on whose sufferance he lives." Thus, for Gandhiji freedom of an individual is comprehensive in concern with the society he lives in; the society must be non-violent.

Gandhian Anarchy

Anarchy in Greek means 'without rulers'. Gandhi's vision of anarchy was simply 'a society without hierarchy' and a society that is non-violent and self-managed.

If everybody turns non-violent, sees one's freedom with the freedom of society, abolishes hierarchy, abides by the ethics and principles suggested by Gandhiji in chapter 1, then an anarchist society could possibly flourish. This will lead to '*swaraj*' or 'self-rule'/ 'autonomy'.

The 'state' at present is created on the basis that people are violent and they constantly infringe on other's freedom, and thus need to be ruled. However, in Gandhian anarchy state, all is different, because individuals have souls.

> "The individual has a soul, but as the state is a soulless machine, it can never be weaved from violence to which it owes its very existence,"
>
> —*Mahatma Gandhi*

Gandhian Democracy

Democracy is the government of people with possible justice and freedom for every citizen. However, according to Gandhiji, "Democracy must be in essence. . . meaning the art and science of mobilizing the entire physical, economic and spiritual resource of all the nations' sections of people in the service of common good of all". And the common good of all can only be certain when every individual is aware of his or her responsibilities, is disciplined and dedicated to the moral and ethical values. In essence, Gandhian democracy is based on service and sacrifice *via* moral obligations or grassroot spiritual ethics. The spirit of democracy cannot be imposed from without; it has to come from within.

Gandhian Nationalism

"My idea of nationalism is that my country may become free, that if need be the whole of the country may die, so that the human race may live. There is no room for race hatred here. Let that be our nationalism," said Gandhiji.[1]

According to Pandit Nehru, Gandhiji's nationalism had a certain world outlook and was entirely free from any aggressive intent. (*The Discovery of India.* p.426).

Gandhian Utopia

The ideal citizen will be an educated one and be an industrious, self-respecting, generous individual living in a small community. The community will be based on *sarvodaya* model and non-violence. In an ideal state of Gandhiji, there will be federated independent village republics known in India as '*Panchayats*'; this in other words is decentralization.

Gita/Bhagwad Gita

Summary of Bhagwad Gita:

> "Your right is to work only,
> But never to its fruits;
> Let not the fruits of action be thy motive,
> Nor let thy attachment be to inaction."

> "You come empty handed, you will leave empty handed. What is yours today, belonged to someone else yesterday, and will belong to someone else the day after tomorrow. So, whatever you do, do it as a dedication to God!"

Teachings of Bhagwad Gita

(i) Do your duty to the best of your ability with mind attached to the lord. Remain calm in both success and failure.

(ii) All works are done by the forces (or *Gunas*) of Nature. Due to ignorance, people assume themselves to be the doer and suffer from Karmic bondage. We all are just a divine instrument and should help each other.

(iii) Self-knowledge removes all our past *karma* and demonic qualities; therefore, is the best purifier.

(iv) Giving up the feeling of doership and ownership is difficult to attain with selfless service which leads to self-knowledge, faith, deep devotion and *Mukti*.

(v) One who sees God everywhere and in everything and sees everything in God, is not away from god, and god is not away from that person. Such a person loves and hates no one.

Grassroot Spirituality

It is next to *dharma* and yet not institutionalized into a religion. It is firm faith in being a god's child and a good soul in the society. It is also treating mother earth as organic and harmonizing with nature.

Hindu and Hinduism

'Hindu is a term popularized by the Arabs referring to all the people living across the river Indus which is referred to as 'Sindhu' in Hindi and Sanskrit. Originally, Hindu is a secular term which used to describe all inhabitants of the Indian sub-continent irrespective of their religious affiliations. The term Hinduism came as late as in 1830s to denote the culture and religion of the high-caste Brahmans in contrast to other religions.

Human and Nature

We, as humans, exist in nature and there is nature because in that we exist.

Indian anthropology starts with this ancient Indian proverb – '*Jaan hai to jahaan hai*', i.e. because there is vital life force, the world exists; '*Aur jahaan mein hi jaan hai*', i.e. and within the world only, exists the vital life force. Thus, physical and environment go hand in hand and we must approach it as such if we are to reach any comprehensive resolution on peace.

This concept of 'Human and Nature' is necessary for peace

because for peace to prevail at all levels, one has to feel peace within himself/herself. That is the task of an individual for himself/herself by being in tune with the environment around and deriving his personal peace through his harmonious relationship with his surroundings. For example, make the dwelling efficient without worrying about the riches and poor; develop the trait in your character that is humane and to your most liking; most of all find your place in the society, accept it and move on ahead.

Interestingly, this very same concept is also inherent among the Natives of North America.

Humanity

In simple terms, humanity is revivifying the 'human and nature' relationship. Anything far removed is not humane.

Karmayoga

It is essentially Acting, or Doing one's duties in life as per his/her *dharma* or duty, without concern of results — a sort of constant sacrifice of action to the Supreme. It is action performed without thought of gain. *Karmayoga* as teaching was passed on from Lord Krishna to Arjuna during the battle of *dharma* fought in Kurukshetra in Bhagwad Gita.

Mother Nature/Prakriti

Mother nature is a feminine concept in Indian thought, *prakriti*. In general, who can be more closer to nature than the creature that abides by nature's cyclical periods for majority of life; in return communing with the ups and downs of her emotional and spiritual plane of consciousness.

Vandana Shiva is described by Rangan as "the best known Indian (and Third-World) ecofeminist in the world today," due in large part to "her repeated and wide spread narration of the Chipko story".[2]

Vandana Shiva, a physicist and an ecofeminist, maintains that women are the custodians of *Prakriti*, nature or the feminine principle, which is the manifestation of *Shakti*, the divine feminine creative energy of the cosmos.[3]

Shiva suggests that in accordance with *Shakti* and *Prakriti*, women were venerated, yet in Brahminical Hindu Tradition, men's fear of *Shakti* is a major reason for the subordination of women.[4]

Non-Violence

Non-violence has one meaning when it is approached as a phenomenon; and yet entirely another meaning when approached as a philosophy.

> *Non-Violence as a phenomenon or Static Non-Violence* – Non-violence as a phenomenon is a theoretical construct with its obvious inherent domains and constraints of not inflicting injury whether that be physical, verbal, emotional etc. It is also an armchair advocacy of non-violence to which always the other should adhere. Thus, it is static in the time and space continuum.
>
> *Non-Violence as a philosophy or Dynamic Non-Violence* – Praxis of non-violence in everyday life is the non-violence philosophy. Its quantum characteristics of inter-influence and inter-annihilation with other forms of violence including philosophy of violence render it dynamic non-violence.

Organic-Sustainable economic model — See Sarvodaya

Pacifism

Pacifism is love of peace and hatred of war.

Peace

Peace when explored as a concept is far different than when it is sought as a path on which to embark one's journey of life.

> *Peace as a concept* – Peace as a theoretical construct has

obvious inherent domains. Peace refers to that moment of non-violence which is absolved in the absence of violence and aggression. Peace is required at all levels; within an individual, family, community, society, nation and world. Peace is also required in all spheres of being — physical, mental, emotional and spiritual. Peace prevails harmony in such that we co-exist.

Peace as a journey – Peace as a journey can not be a theoretical construct because it is not a theory It is a praxis of living *via* non-violence means. In its own entirety, peace as a journey provides peace as means and peace as an end.

Progress/Evolution

Sometimes progress is confused with evolution, so it is necessary to explain them separately.

Progress – The denotation is to move forward and gain. Connotation is a step toward efficiency. Neither the step nor the progress itself is necessarily toward humanity. Thus, in order to attain peace, the step toward efficiency must be based on humane values, keeping in consideration the 'Human and Nature Relationship'.

Evolution – It is simply to grow. Growing doesn't have to be in the path of progression or efficiency. It may be positive or negative.

Evolve as Entirety – Move forward towards humanity as a whole – not only as an individual or family or community or society or nation or a social or an economic or a political entity– but each and everyone of us with similar basic universal ethics/ values of humanity as mentioned in chapter 1 sought by Gandhiji and also sought by Rosa Parks in chapter 6.

Religion

Religion is not external. It is simple faith in god and living in the presence of god. According to Gandhiji religion means faith in a future life, in truth and *Ahimsa*... Religion is a matter of heart. In Hinduism, there is no equivalent of religion. (For more explanation, see *Dharma*.) And Hinduism is not a religion. Hinduism is '*dharma*'. Since '*dharma*' is — that which upholds or sustains the positive order of things: the nation, the community, the family and ultimately even the universe — Hinduism is wordly.

Resistance

In the context of non-violence philosophy, resistance must also be of non-violent nature. *Satyagraha* which means the "force contained in truth and love", is that non-violent resistance. The philosophy of *satyagraha* requires that a person who decided to break the law considered unjust must accept the consequences of that decision also.

Sarvodaya

It is a term meaning 'universal uplift' or 'progress of all'. The term was title of his 1908 translation of John Ruskin's tract on political economy.[5]

Gandhian philosophy of *Sarvodaya* — welfare of all — is based on the ancient scriptures and tradition of India. It refers to uplifting of all. It also gives the meaning "good of all", 'service to all' and 'welfare of all' etc. It is a sort of Gandhian socialism that leads to classless and casteless society.

Satyagraha

It is a Sanskrit word. *Satya* means 'truth' and *'agraha'* means 'insistence' or 'hold firmly to'. Therefore, *satyagraha* is simply 'holding onto the truth'. Open non-violent protests or hunger strikes are such examples of *satyagraha*. However, it is not that simple, there are some principles to abide by as suggested by Gandhiji. Some of them are non-violence, non-stealing, body-labour or bread labour, control of the palate, economic strategy such as boycotts (*swadeshi*) etc. and most of all fearlessness. See chapter 8.

Smarpan Meditation

Smarpan is a Sanskrit word meaning surrender/giving yourself completely. *Smarpan* meditation is a practice which unites us with the Universal Energy.

Social-moral Order

It is an intertwined process of Gandhian non-violence axioms pertaining to spirituality and or humanity.

(i) Stern discipline with firm and loving guidance.
(ii) Responsibility for one's actions.
(iii) Education.
(iv) Self-reliance.
(v) Communication.
(vi) Growing together with one's family and dear ones.
(vii) Vow of poverty (the type of vow of poverty explained in chapter 1.).
(viii) Vow of celibacy (refer to chapter 9 for details).
(ix) Truth
(x) Fearlessness

Sustainable Development — See Development

Ultimate Freedom with Ultimate Responsibility

Ultimate freedom comes with ultimate responsibility.

If one indulges in free-will, one must accept responsibility for the consequences of his/her acts. Who is to judge — the person with higher social status, a virgin with divine beauty, or a person with a lot of money? We are all humans and are therefore, subjective. Best judge of one's actions is the person himself/herself. Keeping in perspective, humanity as last recourse, one must pursue the act of freedom with such responsibility that it minimizes infringing on someone else's freedom.

John Locke, one of the most influential English physician and philosopher 'argued that they [people] should be free to exercise their rights without hindrance or regulation as long as they did not interfere with the rights of others.[6] In case that is not possible, compromise is called in place.

Due to our quantum nature, inter-dependency refrains us from absolutist behaviour, i.e. every single, micro or macro, action brings about an equal and opposite reaction. Whenever, one exercises his/her rights, he/she will definitely interfere with the rights of some others in some negligible or extreme measure. Not exercising is not the answer, nonetheless, one may exercise his/her rights in matter of degrees and to a certain extent. A matter of degrees and a certain extent are the determining nature of compromise.

Compromising is not 'giving in', instead it is exploring the limitations of one's freedom; within the domains of which the limitations one suffers no consequences of exercising freedom.

Violence

Violence refers to abusive behaviour whether that be physical, verbal, emotional, etc. that necessarily infringes on another's rights and freedom.

World Federation

According to the non-violence advocate, Gandhiji, there is no room for armies in a world federation. He believed in the inevitable possibility of a world federation which he said will happen once the nations will renounce violence towards each other and learn to live in peace. This will create voluntary interdependence of states and nations.

Notes

1. Nehru, Jawaharlal, *Nehru on Gandhi: A selection, arranged in the order of events, from the writings and speeches of Jawaharlal Nehru.* The John Day Company: New York, USA: 1948. p. 28-29.
2. Rangan, Haripriya. *Of Myths and Monuments.* New York, Verso: 2000. p.32

3. Shiva, Vandana. *Staying Alive: Women, Ecology and Development*. Kali for Women, New Delhi: 1988.
4. Mawdsley, Emma, "After Chipko: From Environmental to Region in Uttaranchal". *Journal of Peasant Studies*. 25 (4): 36-54. 1998.
5. Wikipedia online.
6. Leon P. Baradat, (4th edition) *Political Ideologies: Their Origins and Impact*. Prentice Hall, Englewood Cliff., New Jersey: 1991. p.60

3

Gandhiji : The Internationalist

> As an heir, even though he were heir to the treasure of all the world, nevertheless does not possess his property before he has come of age, so even the richest personality is nothing before he has chosen himself, and on the other hand even what one might call the poorest personality is everything when he has chosen himself; for the great thing is not to be this or that but to be oneself, and this everyone can be if he wills it.
>
> He who regards life ethically sees the universal, and he who lives ethically expresses the universal in his life, he makes himself the universal man, not by divesting himself of his concretion, for then he becomes nothing, but by clothing himself with it and permeating it with the universal. For the universal man is not a phantom, but every man as such is the universal man, that is to say, to every man the way is assigned by which he becomes the universal man. . . He who lives ethically labours to become the universal man.
>
> —*Kierkegaard*[1]

Interestingly and undoubtedly Gandhiji's lifestyle overlaps many other great personalities in the world simply because Gandhiji was a universal person and an internationalist.

At micro level he harmonized his home life with his wife and children which became his stepping stones toward 'journey of peace'.

At macro level he moved the masses. It is quite needless to say that Gandhiji alone shook the British Empire and brought it to its knees. Although there are arguments that British Empire was more afraid of the constant abrupt riots all over India, nevertheless, British Empire knew very well how to encounter violence with coercion and yet more violence, but what scared the Empire was Gandhian non-violence.

At micro-level, Gandhiji started with purifyıng himself.

In the course of history, there have been countless cases where the 'man of the house' left home and went astray to seek peace and enlightenment and rightfully those men found peace and enlightenment. Along the same paradigm, Gandhiji found peace and enlightenment, but he never left home and he never denounced his worldly responsibilities. On the contrary, he synchronized his mind and soul with his wife and they together synchronized that same mind and soul with their children. These were the stepping stones for Gandhiji toward 'journey of peace'.

As a result, the peace and enlightenment perceived and attained was, in turn, shared with the world and that at a vast level.

Gandhiji shared his enlightenment further with his friends, neighbours, his associates and basically anyone he came in contact with. This answered at least one question to the pondering mind of Pandit Nehru as to why people whom Gandhiji encountered became spiritually enlightened. In this case, one might wonder then why Nehruji, a dear friend of Gandhiji, did not become spiritually enlightened himself considering his countless encounters with Gandhiji. The answer is simple, Nehruji was not seeking spiritual enlightenment; he was a simple man, who was politically driven and British-system-dazzled who just wanted to see the free India and perhaps even rule it, which he did as the first Prime Minister of Independent India.

Nehruji wasn't the only one, some other followers of Gandhiji weren't famous for spiritual enlightenment either, such as Nelson Mandela, Indira Gandhi, Bhagat Singh, whereas Mother Teresa, Vinobha Bhave, Bayard Rustin and Martin Luther King Jr. were known to be spiritual.

And there are personalities like Rosa Parks who was never in direct contact with Gandhiji and yet reflected similar ethics, discipline, values and personality traits. Rabindernath Tagore is another such personality.

Gandhiji and Rabindernath Tagore

> Tagore and Gandhi have undoubtedly been the two outstanding and dominating figures of India in this first half of the twentieth century. It is instructive to compare and contrast them. No two persons could be so different from one another in their make-up or temperaments. Tagore, the aristocratic artist, turned democrat with proletarian sympathies, represented essentially the cultural tradition of India, the tradition of accepting life in the fullness thereof and going through it with song and dance. Gandhi, more a man of the people, almost the embodiment of the Indian peasant, represented the other ancient tradition of India, that of renunciation and asceticism. And yet Tagore was primarily the man of thought, Gandhi of concentrated and ceaseless activity. Both, in their different ways, had a world outlook, and both were at the same time wholly India. They seemed to represent different but harmonious aspects of India and to complement one another.[2]

According to Pandit Nehru, the first Prime Minister of Independent India, the personality of Gandhi and Tagore was quite similar. Born and raised in west Bengal, Tagore held Nobel peace prize in literature for his book entitled '*Geetanjali*'. Geetanjali is a compilation of spiritual poems that are timeless and religion-less. Tagore also wrote national anthem of India upon request. So, yes! Tagore had that encompassing outlook which he applied to his writings and songs. When he wrote National Anthem, he encompassed the outlook of an entire country. When he composed poems in *Geetanjali*, he encompassed the world outlook of spirituality void of time, religion, politics, geography, history, etc.

Thus, their worldly outlook and their ability to be inclusive or encompassing breaking down the intangible man-made barriers of religion, geography and history, etc. have rendered their philosophies timeless. Another remarkable similarity in tneir personalities was that both lived and practised their views and teachings, i.e. praxis. This made their outlook harmonious.

Satyagraha and Fearlessness

One striking resemblance in their harmonious outlook is the innate acceptance of oneself and trust in oneself, i.e. saying the truth as is, leading to the concept of 'no fear'. Though Tagore didn't emphasize on the concept of 'no fear' explicitly, Gandhi verbalized it through '*satyagraha*'.

> It was Gandhi's *satyagraha*, which means holding onto truth. . .
>
> Mahatma Gandhi organized a Satyagraha Sabha of those who were prepared to break chosen laws and thus court imprisonment. This was quite a novel idea then, and many of us were excited but many shrank back. Today it is the most commonplace of occurrences, and for most of us it has become a fixed and regular part of our lives!
>
> As usual with him, Gandhi sent a courteous appeal and warning to the Viceroy. When he saw that the British government was determined to pass the law in spite of the opposition of a united India, he called for an All India day of mourning, a hartal, a stoppage of business, and meetings on the first Sunday after the Bills became law. This was to inaugurate the Satyagraha movement, and so Sunday, April 6, 1919, was observed as the Satyagrah Day All over the country, in town and village. It was the first all-India demonstration of the kind, and it was a wonderfully impressive one, in which all kinds of people and communities joined. Those of us who had worked for this hartal were amazed at its success. . .
>
> A week before April 6, Delhi, mistaking the date, had observed the hartal on the previous Sunday, March 31. Those were days of an amazing comradeship and good will among the Hindus and Moslems of Delhi, and the remarkable sight was witnessed of Swami Shraddhanand, a great leader of the Arya Samaj, addressing huge audiences in the famous Jama Masjid of Delhi.[3]

Satyagraha in Hindi literally means determination for truth, i.e. persistence for truth. In general, people give up the truth or lure away from it in various cases such as coercion as in colonialism, coercion by gangs, peer pressure, money, material gain etc. Gandhi, being one of the best barristers, saw through that. He simplified the defence act and started preparing for it at its own level.

It was the entire colonial regime that was the culprit. The culprit used methods to envelope the general public in its own made-up laws and issued harsh punishment in case of non-obedience. The general public was well aware of this. Gandhiji simply brought out in the open the widespread awareness and showed people a way out of their own mind-block. Gandhiji showed people how they were imprisoned inside their minds. He also realized that the colonists were seeking weaknesses among Indians, heightening those weaknesses and using the resulting unrest to divide Indians and thus gaining more control over them.

Harijans — The People of God

One such weakness he recognized was '*untouchability*'. He saw this as an advantage to free India in terms of national unity.

> Apart from the fundamental objective of the Congress – the freedom of India – and the method of peaceful action, the principal planks of the Congress were national unity, which involved the solution of the minority problems, and the raising of the depressed classes and the ending of the curse of untouchability.[4]

In other words, Gandhiji's strategy was such that whatever he saw as the weakness, he tried to remove it or at least lessen it. *This is undoubtedly the thinking of a barrister.*

For example, as preparing for the court date, a lawyer necessarily advises the defendant to dress nice, act gentle and polite and tries to find justifiable plausible causes for the defendant's behaviours at the time of the execution of crime. Regardless of whether, the crime is solved or not, the party that, comparatively, appears to be closer to solving, wins the game.

Gandhiji coined the term '*harijans*' for untouchables. *Harijans* means 'people of god' in Hindi. In Indian thought, this is appealing to Indians at a spiritual level. Thus, Gandhiji rendered strength to the weakness created by the British Empire and he did it in a most peaceful way. He did not react to the weakness but merely took a proactive approach and dealt with it all the way from bottomup, i.e. from social reform to setting quota system at political and economic level.

Nevertheless, there was something different about Gandhiji, the barrister. As he set out to prepare a good stage to defend India, he actually started a bottom up approach of cleaning up the act. He started with himself first, then his family, then his friends, community etc. and finally the nation.

Critics as well as his followers such as Bayard Rustin argue that Gandhiji's vision of non-violence philosophy got limited to India's freedom and thus, lost its worldly approach. Whereas Gandhiji, as a lawyer, focused on India's freedom because it was much needed at the moment and because it hit home for him. And once he set on this task, the task itself became endless because he saw a lot within India that needed to reform which consumed him.

One for Oneself because Truth Triumphs

There is something else essential, another necessary basic principle that he came across while on his journey of non-violence that everyone will have to stand-up for himself/herself. This means embark on the journey of peace. If it is your war then it is essentially you who must confront it, you may not ask someone else to confront it for you. Indians needed freedom for Indians and India, Gandhiji showed the Indians to stand-up for themselves first and then for India. He awakened the people from within, for which reason he was, and, is referred to as a 'Mahatma', a great soul.

> What was his idea of India which he was setting out to mold according to his own wishes and ideals? "I shall work for an India in which the poorest shall feel that it is their country, in whose making they have an effective voice, an India in which there shall be no high class and low class of people, an India in which all communities shall live in perfect harmony. . . There can be no room in such an India for the curse of untouchability . . . for the curse of intoxicating drinks and drugs. . . Women who will enjoy the same rights as men. . . This is the India of my dreams."
>
> Proud of his Hindu inheritance as he was, he tried to give to Hinduism a kind of universal attire and included all religions within the fold of truth. He refused to narrow his cultural inheritance. "Indian culture," he wrote, is neither Hindu, Islamic

> nor any other, wholly. It is a fusion of all." Again he said: "I want the culture of all lands to be blown about my house as freely as possible. But I refuse to be blown off my feet by any. I refuse to live in other people's houses an interloper, a beggar or a slave." Influenced by modern thought currents, he never let go of his roots and clung to them tenaciously.[5]

An admirable soul who — reached out to all types of people regardless of class, creed, religion etc. – was influenced as much by the modern undercurrents as well as grounded by his cultural roots. He had a total acceptance of himself. Instead of questioning what he had no control over, he gained control over himself and he became the change he sought in others.

Gandhi included all religions within the fold of truth which is reflected in the Indian Emblem whose slogan reads 'Truth Triumphs'.

> Gandhi was essentially a man of religion, a Hindu to the innermost depths of his being, and yet his conception of religion had nothing to do with any dogma or custom or ritual.* (p.21, Nehru on Gandhi) [Gandhi told the Federation of International Fellowships in January 1928 that "after long study and experience I have come to these conclusions, that: (1) all religions are true, (2) all religions have some error in them, (3) all religions are as dear to me as my own Hinduism. My veneration for other faiths is the same as for my own faith. Consequently, the thought of conversion is impossible. . . Our prayer for others ought never to be: 'God! Give them the light thou hast given to me!' but: 'Give them all the light and truth they need for their highest development!'"
>
> He was basically concerned with his firm belief in the moral law, which he calls the Law of Truth or Love. Truth and non-violence appear to him to be the same thing or different aspects of one and the same thing, and he uses these words almost interchangeably.
>
> Claiming to understand the spirit of Hinduism, he rejects every text or practise which does not fit in with his idealist interpretation of what it should be, calling it an interpolation or a subsequent accretion. "I decline to be a slave," he has said, "to precedents or practise I cannot understand or defend on a moral basis." And so in practise he is singularly free to take the path of his choice, to life and action, subject only to

> the overriding consideration of the moral law as he conceives this to be. Whether that philosophy is right or wrong may be argued, but he insists on applying the same fundamental yardstick to everything, and himself specially.[6]

Upholding of *Truth* or *Love* as in *duty* and *righteousness*, is an embedded concept of *Dharma*[7] in Indian thought. *Dharma* is void of religion but essential food for spirituality and inner awakening. Thus, Gandhiji's world look on universal law of truth or love was the take on *Dharma*. Gandhiji's look was always worldly. People who argue otherwise have missed the essential steps of Gandhiji's philosophy.

One of the main steps was and is that the change starts with oneself. He was Indian by birth and nationality. He was nurtured in bare Indian thought. Even though, he travelled outside of India, the problems he faced and conquered were essentially to do with his *Indianness*. He wanted to make a change, so, he started with himself as an Indian, a process which he involved other Indians in. 'Independence of India' was an uppermost world issue at the moment and he prepared for that – Indians for the freedom of India.

A precise analogy is Mandela's movement for the freedom of South-Africa. Mandela followed the essential steps of the non-violence philosophy of Mahatma Gandhi:

(i) *Satyagraha* – he went to prison for his naked beliefs of seeking freedom for South Africa.

(ii) Mandela became the change he wanted to see in others.

(iii) He appealed to his people and united them by attempting to remove their weaknesses and therefore, strengthening them.

(iv) He approached with non-violence to seek in return a non-violent free South Africa.

In other words, Nelson Mandela became what he sought in his opponent. Just as Gandhiji became what he sought in British Raj. Another example is the civil movement of Black African Americans in USA. In the due process, they also became what they sought in their opponent or the oppressor. And they succeeded.

The point is that one has to stand up for himself and shed any fear. Indians stood up to free India. Black South Africans stood up to free South Africa (without apartheid) and Black African-Americans stood up for the civil rights of Black African-Americans. You want it, you stand up for it.

Standing up for oneself has another element to it – truth. When you stand up for rights/beliefs, you are standing up for your truth. And truth is extremely simple and transparent compared to lies. You lie the first time because you don't want to tell the truth for some reason. Eventually, you lie again to cover up the first lie. Eventually it becomes a pattern. Lies weave a web of deception around the liar whereas truth does not require that. Such is Gandhiji's *Satyagraha*. In simple terms, *Satyagraha* is 'persistence for truth'. In order to prepare oneself for *Satyagraha*, one has to give up all the lies, deception and secrets. This helps to bring truth in the open.

And why one must hold *Satyagraha* for his/her truth/*satya*? Because truth is relative and the total persistence force of the truth comes from itself. Therefore, the oppressed must shed the path of lies, deception and secrets in order to make his/her truth transparent. This is an individual approach, an approach that starts from within and from oneself.

In this sense, Gandhiji at first put himself on the path of truth and then put Indians on the path of truth before suggesting *Satyagraha* to them. This was the logic of a lawyer born and bred in India during his early days, in a land of spirituality. Spirituality was an innate part of Gandhiji and his lawyer personality reasoned it so that the Indians will stand up for their own rights in their own manner. Thus, explains his nationalism.

Since spirituality is grassroot and universal, it can be postulated at the world level. This explains Gandhiji's world outlook.

His friends and people in general saw different aspects of his personality.

World Federation

> Gandhi gave a turn to our nationalist movement which lessened the feelings of frustration and bitterness. Those feelings

> continued, but I do not know of any other nationalist movement which has been so free from hatred. Gandhi was an intense nationalist; he was also, at the same time, a man who felt he had a message not only for India but for the world, and he ardently desired world peace. His nationalism, therefore, had a certain world outlook and was entirely free from any aggressive intent. Desiring the independence of India, he had come to believe that a world federation of interdependent states was the only right goal, however distant that might be. He had said: "My idea of nationalism is that my country may become free, that if need be the whole of the country may die, so that the human race may live. There is no room for race hatred here. Let that be our nationalism." And again: "I do want to think in terms of the whole world. My patriotism includes the good of mankind in general. Therefore, my service of India includes the service of humanity. . . Isolated independence is not the goal of the world states. It is voluntary interdependence. The better mind of the world desires today not absolutely independent states, warring one against another, but a federation of friendly, interdependent states. The consummation of that event may be far off. I want to make no grand claim for our country. But I see nothing grand or impossible about our expressing our readiness for universal interdependence rather than independence. I desire the ability to be totally independent without asserting the independence."[8]

According to Pandit Nehru, Gandhiji gave a turn to our nationalist movement. . ., however, Gandhiji was a down to earth pragmatic soul. He improvised the evolution of his search for truth or spiritual progress or charity or whatever one may choose to call it. The point is that, at first, he became the change he sought in others, and then he influenced, through his actions and not only through his words, his friends, his neighbours, his neighbourhood, community, society etc. Following the same path of reasoning, he gave a turn to the nationalist movement and made it a world movement.

Let's analyze this again. His outlook started with himself and then expanded outwards without any bounds. Let's suppose that he had started with an outlook that was already a 'society outlook' or a 'national outlook'. Such an outlook would require domains and thus will be limited. Gandhiji's outlook started with an individual – the minuscule particle in the making of any group formations such as society, nation, world, etc. Another essential part of Gandhiji's outlook is that he applied the concept of 'Man and Nature' originated in Indian thought. Consequently, Gandhiji's vision of a good soul will be an individual who is in harmony with nature and innately spiritual.

Such grassroot spiritual individuals will form grassroot spiritual nations and so on. On other hand, if one describes an abstract notion of spiritual society and expects all individuals to conform to its rules and regulations, it can be problematic.

Simply put, a grassroot spiritual individual or a Gandhian is able to be anywhere and still harmony will prevail.

Gandhiji and Nationalism

Nehru mentioned that Gandhiji gave a turn to our nationalist movement, in fact, Gandhiji had simply moved on from 'nation' level to the 'world' level.

It is interesting to note that a large majority seems to think that Gandhiji was an intense nationalist. In fact, Gandhi was a free spirit open to the world. Then why was he considered an intense nationalist?

Gandhi was born in India. He grew up amongst Indian rituals and ceremonies. He had an Indian wife and his family was in India while he was abroad studying/working. When his rights were infringed and he was discriminated, it was due to his Indian look and his *Indianness*. However, he did not see his *Indianness* as a weakness because he was an achiever and *Indianness* was just something that he had – perhaps an asset that flourished the essence of his being. He was set apart because of his Indian attire. Nevertheless, he himself never experienced any difficulties because he was Indian. He actually turned his *Indianness* to his advantage. In times of difficulties he turned to his *Indianness*. This is one of the reasons why Gandhiji tried to be the best Indian himself at first and then tried to show the other Indians to be the best that they are. His '*Indianness*' or 'Indian nationalism' is a look from the outside. This 'Indian nationalism' is a concept of the western world-nation system.

The Indians related to Gandhiji instantly because of their shared heritage. The others related to Gandhiji because they saw a free-spirited great soul and they wanted to be like him to be able to achieve at such a great extent as he did. For example, Bayard Rustin and Martin Luther King Jr. visited India to feel and experience the place where such a great soul as Gandhiji roamed freely and attained freedom. Nelson Mandela also adopted Gandhian philosophy of non-violence to free South Africa. So, as non-Indians saw the world look in Gandhiji, Indians saw that world look also but in an innate Indian. In other words, Gandhiji's nationalism was just something innate and therefore, Gandhiji was not a nationalist but a product of Indian nationalism in time and geography continuum. Gandhiji himself was beyond any nationalism – a free spirited great soul.

Being a lawyer, he understood the nature of British empire seeking markets and creating economic dependence of India. Keeping the current dynamics in perspective, he emphasized interdependent states which meant rolling of economy, keeping India together and post-Independent India as an equal partner in the world economy and politics.

But remember that the world outlook of Gandhiji was rooted in grassroot spiritual individuals. He simply delivered the means of will to the demoralized, backward and broken-up Indians.

> "It was this extraordinary stiffening up of the masses that filled us with confidence. A demoralized, backward, and broken-up people suddenly straightened their backs and lifted their heads and took part in disciplined, joint action on a country-wide scale. This action itself, we felt, would give irresistible power to the masses. We ignored the necessity of thought behind the action; we forgot that without a conscious ideology and objective the energy and enthusiasm of the masses must end largely in smoke. To some extent the revivalist element in our movement carried us on; a feeling that non-violence as conceived for political or economic movements or for righting wrongs was a new message which our people were destined to give to the world. We became victims to the curious illusion of all peoples and all nations that in some way they are a chosen race. Non-violence was the moral equivalent of war, and of all violent struggle. It was not merely an ethical alternative, but it was effective also. Few of us, I think, accepted Gandhiji's old ideas about machinery and modern civilization. We thought that even he looked upon them as Utopian and as largely inapplicable to modern conditions. Certainly most of us were

> not prepared to reject the achievements of modern civilization, although we may have felt that some variation to suit Indian conditions was possible. Personally, I have always felt attracted toward big machinery and fast travelling. Still, there can be no doubt that Gandhiji's ideology influenced many people and made them critical of the machine and all its consequences. So, while some looked to the future, others looked back to the past. And, curiously, both felt that the joint action they were indulging in was worthwhile, and this made it easy to bear sacrifice and face self-denial. [Toward Freedom, p. 70-5][9]

Non-Violence Infinitely Superior to Violence

Through his long-term vision acquired after critical reasoning from grassroot spiritual perspective, Gandhiji proposed his Doctrine of the Sword to the mobilized public whom Gandhiji considered soldiers for non-violence, "the moral equivalent of war". Though Gandhiji preferred violence to cowardice when it came to defending oneself or one's honour; however, he held non-violence infinitely superior to violence.

> . . . "In a famous article - "The Doctrine of the Sword" — he had written in 1920 :
>
> I do believe that when there is only a choice between cowardice and violence, I would advise violence. . . I would rather have India resort to arms in order to defend her honour than she should in a cowardly manner become or remain a helpless victim to her own dishonour. But I believe that non-violence is infinitely superior to violence, forgiveness is more manly than punishment.
>
> Forgiveness adorns a soldier. But abstinence is forgiveness only when there is power to punish; it is meaningless when it pretends to proceed from a helpless creature. A mouse hardly forgives a cat when it allows itself to be torn to pieces by her. . . But I do not believe India to be helpless, I do not believe myself to be a helpless creature. . .
>
> Let me not be misunderstood. Strength does not come from physical capacity. It comes from an indomitable will. . .
>
> I am not a visionary. I claim to be a practical idealist. The religion of non-violence is not meant merely for the *rishis* and saints. It is meant for the common people as well. Non-violence

> is the law of our species as violence is the law of the brute. The spirit lies dormant in the brute, and he knows no law but that of physical might. The dignity of man requires obedience to a higher law – to the strength of the spirit.
>
> I have therefore, ventured to place before India the ancient law of self-sacrifice. For *Satyagraha* and its offshoots, non-co-operation and civil resistance, are nothing but new names for the law of suffering. The *rishis* who discovered the law of non-violence in the midst of violence were greater geniuses than Newton. They were themselves greater warriors than Wellington. Having themselves known the use of arms, they realized their uselessness and taught a weary world that its salvation lay not through violence be through non-violence.
>
> Non-violence in its dynamic condition means conscious suffering. It does not mean meek submission to the will of the evildoer, but it means the putting of one's whole soul against the will of the tyrant. Working under the law of our being, it is possible for a single individual to defy the whole might of an unjust empire to save his honour, his religion, his soul, and lay the foundation for that empire's fall or regeneration.
>
> And so I am not pleading for India to practise non-violence because it is weak. I want her to practise non-violence being conscious of her strength and power... I want India to recognize that she has a soul that cannot perish, and that can rise triumphant above any physical weakness and defy the physical combination of a whole world...
>
> I isolate this non-co-operation from Sinn Feinism, for it is so conceived as to be incapable of being offered side by side with violence. But I invite even the school of violence to give this peaceful non-co-operation a trial. It will not fail through its inherent weakness. It may fail because of poverty of response. Then will be the time for real danger. The high-souled men, who are unable to suffer national humiliation any longer, will want to vent their wrath. They will take to violence. So far as I know, they must perish without delivering themselves or their country from the wrong. If India takes up the doctrine of the sword, she may gain momentary victory. Then India will cease to be the pride of my heart. I am wedded to India because I owe my all to her. I believe absolutely that she has a mission for the world.[10]

The world's largest democracy and a secular nation for all was the mission of Gandhiji's India for the world. For Gandhiji, the spirit of democracy was to emanate from within just as the non-violence doctrine emanated from within the conscious of the soul, the will.

In fact, Gandhiji's theory was quite simple and he abide by very few simple ethics – mainly 'truth *via* transparency' and 'grassroot spirituality'. Keeping his basic assumptions in check, he proceeded to implement his theory, whether in the name of *Satyagraha*, non-violence or propagating Gandhian democracy.

Unlike the notion of western democracy based on numbers and majority, Gandhian democracy was based on service and sacrifice *via* moral obligation or grassroot spiritual ethics. 'Sacrifice' is an ambiguous word. Reflecting on Gandhiji's life experiences and his lectures to masses, the word sacrifice is used commonly and sparingly simultaneously. What Gandhiji meant by sacrifice was a well thought-out action taken under one's will in the defence of one's honour where that honour has to be substantiated – meaning that the honour itself has to be based on the fundamental principles of truth and grassroot spirituality as well.

Making sacrifice by one's free choice for Independence of India is valid, provided that the free India envisioned, in return, retains the right to one's free choice.

Here is another example at an individual level. Let's say that there is a poor couple and both have to work to make ends meet. By all means, yes. However, if the husband is a drunkard, his wife should not sacrifice her hard earnings on his drinking; similarly a husband should not sacrifice his hard earnings on a wife who is not for the welfare of her family and society, etc.

Gandhiji and Democracy

Getting back to the concept of democracy, Gandhiji's notion of democracy not only surpassed western democracy with its sole notion of quantitative methods of measure *via* numbers and masses but it also surpassed communist conception of democracy with its sole notion of quantitative methods of services rendered of masses.

> Gandhiji's conception of democracy has nothing to do with numbers or majority or representation in the ordinary sense. It is based on service and sacrifice, and it uses moral pressure.

> He claims to be "a born democrat." "I make that claim, if complete identification with the poorest of mankind, longing to live no better than they, and a corresponding conscious effort to approach that level to the best of one's ability can entitle one to make it." This is his definition of a democrat. He says further:
>
> Let us recognize the fact that the Congress enjoys the prestige of a democratic character and influence not by the number of delegates and visitors it has drawn to its annual function, but by an ever increasing amount of service it has rendered. Western democracy is on its trial, if it has not already proved a failure. May it be reserved to India to evolve the true science of democracy by giving a visible demonstration of its success. Corruption and hypocrisy ought not to be the inevitable products of democracy, as they undoubtedly are today. Nor is bulk a true test of democracy. True democracy is not inconsistent with a few persons representing the spirit, the hope and the aspirations of those whom they claim to represent. I hold that democracy cannot be evolved by forcible methods. The spirit of democracy cannot be imposed from without; it has to come from within.
>
> This is certainly not western democracy, as he himself says; but, curiously enough, there is some similarity to the communist conception of democracy. A few communists will claim to represent the real needs and desires of the masses, even though the latter may themselves be unaware of them. The similarity, however, is slight and does not take us far; the differences in outlook and approach are far greater, notably in regard to methods and force. . . .

Gandhian democracy cuts rather close to *Gita's* teachings mainly based on '*Karmayoga*'. In short, the emphasis is on performing deeds as one's duty calls and not expect any reward/s in return. If you approach your actions, as stated in *Karmayoga*, your actions will automatically fall under Gandhism whether it is a non-violent march, a *Satyagraha* or a democratic act. This turned Gandhiji into a mystery even to his close ones.

> Democracy demands discipline, tolerance and mutual regard. Freedom demands respect for the freedom of others. In a democracy changes are made by mutual discussion and persuasion and not by violent means. If a Government has not

> got popular support, another government takes its place which commands that popular support. It is only small groups, who know that they cannot get sufficient popular support, that resort to methods of violence, imagining in their folly that they can gain their ends in this way. This is not only utterly wrong but it is also utterly foolish. For the reaction to the violence of the minority, which seeks to coerce the majority, is to provoke the majority into violence against them.[17]

Gandhiji was well aware of minorities in India and minorities' methods. His suggestion to make Jinnah the first Prime Minister arose out of such contemplations while he held the safety and peace of India at his heart.

It remains to ponder whether Gandhiji sided with Muslims or Muslims sided with Gandhiji prior to India's freedom. The answer is simple. A quite large majority of Indian Hindus readopted to the concept of '*dharma*'. Even though '*dharma*' is universal and is an essential part of any religion, perhaps Muslim Brothers masses did not adhere to *dharma* because if they did they would not have approached Gandhiji about their 'minority concerns', but instead they would have dealt with their concerns themselves.

During and after the struggle to free India, Indians still regarded Gandhiji as a Mahatma, a great soul. Critics of Gandhiji and his methods perhaps do not have the determination and indomitable will to follow his ways and methods of *dharma*, *ahimsa* and *satyagraha*.

Dharma, ahimsa and satyagraha are the peaceful means to attain peaceful end. Therefore, peace must be a non-violent journey.

Then, one person, way across Himalayas and past oceans saw the light. He was a visionary.

Gandhiji — A Mystery

Why Gandhiji's ways remained mystery to Pandit Nehru and he often encountered the unknown in Gandhi's eyes is because Nehru failed to comprehend Gandhi's series of logic which Gandhiji 'accommodated' in India's traditional masses whereas Nehru remained encompassed within his own frame of mind. Nehru could not fathom 'accommodating' or 'merging' the logic and system, which on the contrary, Gandhiji accomplished.

For example, Gandhiji regarded 'a wife working shoulder to shoulder with her husband' as a concept of egalitarianism prevalent in the English society, so he set forth within the domains of Indian Thought by educating his wife and teaching all the household chores to all his family members. He also sought to set parallel paradigms amongst his family. And he requested his already willing wife to empower the women of masses in India.

Let's look at the same example from Nehru's perspective. Nehru was brought up in a family that was well-versed in British system and mannerism. His bringing up was more in British mannerism and the Indian traditional elements were suggested here and there, when and where seemed necessary. Nehru's wife, Kamla Nehru, who grew up in an innately, Indian traditional household, had found her husband's ways hard to grasp in the beginning. Because along with British system and mannerism seeped in the British logic and reasoning as well.

This is what was different in Nehruji and Gandhiji. Gandhiji grew up in a balanced Indian traditional home and then he was opened up to the British system, through education at the age of 19; and so he literally witnessed two different logic patterns. Whereas, Nehruji grew up with somewhat innate British logic which was compounded when he left India at the young age of 15 to study sciences in England, however, trained as a barrister afterwards. So, Nehruji always saw and experienced Indian culture from the outside as an attire and this led to the differences in Nehru and Gandhiji as to why Nehruji saw the unknown in Ganhiji's eyes.

Kamla Nehru also served the society and India in general but in a conventional manner. Nehru kept the conventional confines of his society of India to fight under only one pretext, that of demanding India's freedom. Gandhi's pretext was also the same, however, he united the masses of India not to use violence to gain means but united them spiritually and at a down-to-earth grassroot level in a way that their unity, and thus, strength commanded nothing else but freedom. In order to unite the masses of India, he stumbled upon, through his experimentation with his own family and reasoning, the unbreakable bondage of Notoriously Spiritual Indian Thought. Since spirituality is a journey within, innate, which Pandit Nehru did not have and which he often encountered as the unknown staring through Gandhiji's eyes.

> What a problem and a puzzle he has been not only to the British government but to his own people and his closest associates! Perhaps in every other country he would be out of place today, but India still seems to understand, or at least appreciate, the prophetic-religious type of man, talking of sin and salvation and non-violence. Indian mythology is full of stories of great ascetics who, by the rigour of their sacrifices and self-imposed penance, built up a "mountain of merit" which threatened the dominion of some of the lessergods and upset the established order. These myths have come often to my mind when I have watched the amazing energy and inner power of Gandhiji, coming out of some inexhaustible spiritual reservoir. He was obviously not of the world's ordinary coinage; he was minted of a different and rare variety, and often the unknown stared at us through his eyes. (p. 61-63, Nehru on Gandhi)
>
> "Gandhiji is always thinking in terms of personal salvation and of sin, while most of us have society's welfare uppermost in our minds. I find it difficult to grasp the idea of sin, and perhaps it is because of this that I cannot appreciate Gandhiji's general outlook. He is not out to change society or the social structure; he devotes himself to the eradication of sin from individuals. "The follower of *Swadeshi*," he has written, "never takes upon himself the vain task of trying to reform the world, for he believes that the world is moved and always will be moved according to the rules set by God." And yet his is aggressive enough in his attempts to reform the world; but the reform he aims at is individual reform, the conquest over the senses and the desire to indulge them, which is sin. Probably he will agree with the definition of liberty which an able Roman Catholic writer on fascism has given: "Liberty is not more than freedom from the bondage of sin." How almost identical this is with the words of the Bishop of London written two hundred years ago: "The Freedom which Christianity gives is Freedom from the Bondage of sin and Satan and from the Dominion of Men's Lusts and Passions and inordinate Desires." [Toward Freedom, p.313-6][11]

Let's entertain Gandhiji's notion of democracy that is emanated from Gita's teachings, mainly *Karmayoga*. Before any explanations of Gita's teachings and *Karmayoga*, one must understand the notion of religion in India and in Indian Thought.

Religion *vs.* Dharma

In Indian thought, the word 'religion', as understood in the west, does not exist. Hinduism is not just a mere religion, but higher than the institution of religion with a world-look; Hinduism is *Dharma*. In Hindi, the word 'religion' literally translates to '*dharma*', which refers to grassroot spirituality at micro and macro level simultaneously, the binding vital force of 'Indian Thought'.

Dharma is used invariably with many concepts among Indians. For example, righteousness, duty, values, ethics, principles etc. Indians refer to *dharma* in their daily conversation as such:

- You stole from a child?
  Don't you have any *dharma*?
  This implies *dharma* as values.
- How could you turn away a hungry person from your door?
  Don't you have any *dharma*?
  This implies *dharma* as ethics.
- According to *dharma*, one shouldn't shout at elders.
  This implies *dharma* as a principle.
- *Dharma* calls on your duty to take care of your parents in their old age.
  This implies *dharma* as a duty.
- If you don't stand by your family in bad times as well as in good times, it will be '*adharma*' (meaning 'not *dharma*').
  This implies *dharma* as righteousness.

These are just some general examples of *dharma* to point out that '*dharma*' is a vast concept and phenomenon simultaneously, binding human to nature in a serene and just manner.

In essence, *Dharma* is the innate fundamental universal principle of 'human and nature (*prakriti*)' in nature. Nature/*prakriti* is the binding factor of *dharma* to humans. Thus, *dharma* is necessarily grassroot. On the contrary, the institution of religion is not grass-root.

Gandhiji abide by '*dharma*' whereas Nehruji, who was awed by modernity and was caught in the race to modernization, found himself unable to revert back to the very fundamental basics of his own culture because Nehruji didn't know the fundamental basics of Indian Thought since he did not grow up with them.

> "What Religion Means"
>
> "No man can live without religion," Gandhiji has written somewhere. "There are some who in the egotism of their reason declare that they have nothing to do with religion, but that is like a man saying that he breathes, but that he has no nose." Again he says: "My devotion to truth has drawn me into the field of politics; . . . Perhaps it would have been more correct if he had said that most of these people who want to exclude religion from life and politics mean that word "religion" something very different from what he means. It is obvious that he is using it in a sense – probably moral and ethical more than any other – different from that of the critics of religion.
>
> [Toward Freedom, p.243][12]

Nehru appearing though unaware of the concept of '*dharma*' as a translation of the word 'religion', also agrees that Gandhiji's notion of religion is 'probably moral and ethical more than any other'. A glimpse at Gandhiji's journey for truth and his adherence to grass-root spirituality reveals that Gandhiji even saw through religion that it was a manifest of the 'west' and subscribed to its, equivalent in 'Indian Thought' which is '*dharma*'.

Dharma ignites one's soul to its utmost heights of conscience and enlightenment. Based on the very principles of *dharma*, Gandhiji had approached democracy siding with socialism and bypassing democracy.

Gandhiji and Socialism

His "Socialism"

Sometimes he calls himself a socialist, but he uses the word in a sense peculiar to himself which has little or nothing to do with the economic framework of society which usually goes by the name of socialism. Following his lead, a number of prominent Congressmen have taken to the use of that word, meaning thereby a kind of muddled humanitarianism. I know that Gandhiji is not ignorant of the subject, for he has read many books on economics and socialism and even Marxism, and has discussed it with others. But I am becoming more and more convinced that in vital matters the mind by itself does not carry us far.

Gandhiji underwent a tremendous conversion during his early days in South Africa, and this shook him up greatly and altered his whole outlook on life. Since then he has had a fixed basis for all his ideas, and his mind is hardly an open mind. He listens with the greatest patience and attention to people who make new suggestions to him, but behind all his courteous interest one has the impression that one is addressing a closed door. He is so firmly anchored to some ideas that everything else seems unimportant. To insist on other and secondary matters would be a distraction and distortion of the larger scheme. To hold onto that anchor would necessarily result in a proper adjustment of these other matters. If the means are right, the end is bound to be right.

That, I think, is the main background of his thought. He suspects also socialism,. And more particularly Marxism, because of their association with violence. The very words "class war" breathe conflict and violence and are thus repugnant to him. He has also no desire to raise the standards of the masses beyond a certain very modest competence, for higher standards and leisure may lead to self-indulgence and sin. It is bad enough that the handful of the well-to-do are self-indulgent; it would be much worse if their numbers were added to.

That outlook is far removed from the socialistic, or for that matter the capitalistic, as anything can be. To say that science and industrial technique today can demonstrably feed, clothe, and house everybody and raise their standards of living very greatly, if vested interests did not intervene, does not interest him much, for he is not keen on those results, beyond a certain

> limit. The promise of socialism therefore holds no attraction for him, and capitalism is only partly tolerable because it circumscribes the evil. He dislikes both, but puts up with the latter for the present as a lesser evil and as something which exists and of which he has to take cognizance.
>
> . . . He does not want people to make an ideal of ever increasing comfort and leisure, but to think of the moral life, to give up their bad habits, to indulge themselves less and less, and thus to develop themselves individually and spiritually. And those who wish to serve the masses have not so much to raise them materially as to go down themselves to their level and mix with them on equal terms. In so doing inevitably they will help in raising them somewhat. That, according to him, is true democracy.[13]

The very idea that those who wish to serve the masses must get down to the mass level and mix with them to alleviate their standard of life is promoted today as well. Since a very small percentage of the population is elite and the resources are somewhat depleted catering to their self-indulgence and leisure, and therefore, not enough resources are available to alleviate the masses, who have to lessen their standards toward the masses. Simply put, the rich need to become less rich to eradicate poverty.

Henceforth, though implausible, the concept remains, of true democracy according to Gandhiji.

Even though both Gandhiji and Pandit Nehru studied abroad at Oxford, Gandhiji was able to absorb more subtleties of the British system and its culture whereas Pandit Nehru took it at its face value.

It was Gandhiji's ability to penetrate enhanced by his law studies, Gandhiji applied his learnt tactics not only to dismantle India's system but he managed to restructured India's system in such a way that she could withstand British system at all trends and stand up for her own rights and virtues.

Thus, holding certain universal principles true to himself he would get to know the masses, then disengage himself giving himself enough time to bring his theories up to par with the masses. Once done, he would engage with the masses again.

In fact, leaders do this all the time. They hold meetings or focus groups, meet people, get to know their strengths and weaknesses, then make changes in their approach or their system accordingly. This process repeats periodically.

Gandhiji and Dharma

Though the very teachings of *Gita* that influenced him for life and the likes of which he encountered in Ruskin's writings and in Bible, Gandhiji, without a doubt, stuck to his grassroot spirituality and *Karmayoga*. His every outlook and his every action emanated from *Gita's* teachings and *Karmayoga*, so obviously, people he interacted with and influenced also became in tuned with *Gita's* teachings and *Karmayoga*, raising them to higher moral and ethical level.

> Gandhi, for all his rocklike adherence to certain principles, has shown a great capacity to adapt himself to others and to changing circumstances, to take into consideration the strength and weakness of those others, and especially of the mass of the people, and how far they were capable of acting up to the truth as he saw it. But from time to time he pulls himself up, as if he were afraid that he had gone too far in his compromising, and returns to his moorings. In the midst of action, he seems to be in tune with the mass mind, responsive to its capacity and therefore adapting himself to it to some extent; at other times he becomes more theoretical and apparently less adaptable. There is also the same difference observable in his action and his writings. This is confusing to his won people; more so to others who are ignorant of the background in India. How far a single individual can influence a people's thought and ideology it is difficult to say. Some people in history have exerted a powerful influence, and yet it may be that they have emphasized and brought out something that already existed in the mind of the people, or have given clear and pointed expression to the vaguely felt ideas of the age. Gandhi's influence on India's mind has been profound in the present age; how long and in what form it will endure, only the future can show. That influence is not limited to those who agree with him or accept him as a national leader; it extends to those also who disagree with him and criticize him. Very few persons in India accept in its entirety his doctrine of non-violence or

> his economic theories, yet very many have been influenced by them in some way or other. Usually speaking in terms of religion, he has emphasized the moral approach to political problems as well as those of everyday life. The religious background has affected those chiefly who were inclined that way, but the moral approach has influenced other also. Many have been appreciably raised to higher levels or moral an ethical action, and many more have been forced to think at least in those terms, and that thought itself has some effect on action and behaviour. Politics ceases to be just expediency and opportunism, as it usually has been everywhere, and there is a continuous moral tussle preceding thought and action. Expediency, or what appears to be immediately possible and desirable, can never be ignored, but it is toned down by other considerations and a longer view of more distant consequences.
>
> Gandhi's influence in these various directions has pervaded India and left its mark. But it is not because of his non-violence or economic theories that he has become the foremost and most outstanding of India's leaders. To the vast majority of India's people he is the symbol of India determined to be free, of militant nationalism, of a refusal to submit to arrogant might, of never agreeing to anything involving national dishonour. Though many people in India may disagree with him on a hundred matters, though they may criticize him or even part company from him on some particular issues, at a time of action and struggle when India's freedom is at stake, they flock to him again and look up to him as their inevitable leader.[14]

The reason why the masses flocked to him at the time of action and struggle was because he had the mantra that binded the masses – '*dharma*'. His much needed help at the time of the struggle for India's freedom sets an example in itself that *dharma* is fundamental to Indian thought.

> He was a Hindu and an Indian and the greatest in many generations, and he was proud of being a Hindu and an Indian. To him India was dear because she had represented throughout the ages certain immutable truths. But though he was intensely religious and came to be called the Father of the Nation which he had liberated, yet no narrow religious or national bonds confined his spirit. And so he became a great internationalist,

> believing in the essential unity of man, the underlying unity of all religions and needs of humanity, and more specifically devoting himself to the service of the poor distressed and oppressed millions everywhere.[15]

Again Nehru realizes that 'no narrow religion or national bonds confined his spirit. And so he became great internationalist. . ." It was '*dharma*' that rendered Gandhiji 'internationalist', and thus, he was able to unite the masses with the weapon of much tolerance.

> He was great unifier in India who taught us not only bare tolerance of others but the willing acceptance of them as our friends and comrades in common undertakings. He taught us to rise above our little selves and prejudices and to see good in others. His last few months and his very death symbolize to us this message of large hearted tolerance and unity. A little while before he died we pledged ourselves in this before him. We must keep that pledge and remember that India is a common home to all those who live here, to whatever religion they may belong. They are equal sharers in our great inheritance and they have equal rights and obligations. Ours is a composite nation as all great nations must necessarily be. Any narrowness in outlook, any attempt to confine the bounds of this great nation, will be a betrayal to his final lesson to us and will surely lead to disaster and loss of that freedom for which he laboured and which he gained for us in a large measure.[16]

Gandhiji not only united masses of India, but by reflecting on the underlying binding *sutra*, he had an insight into uniting the masses of the world with '*dharma*'. While reading about various spiritual dogmas he remembered that all religions are similarly great and yet have similar errors. '*Dharma*' is a concept that exists in all religions and opens the doors to a 'worldly outlook' rendering everyone a citizen of the world; as democracy pretends to.

Notes

1. Iyer, Raghavan N., *The Moral and Political thought of Mahatma Gandhi*. Oxford University Press, New Delhi. 1973. p. 345.

2. Nehru, Jawaharlal. *The Discovery of India.* Oxford University Press; Centenary edition January 1, 1994. P.342-343.
3. *Ibid.* p. 2-6.
4. *Ibid.* p. 19.
5. *Ibid.* p. 23.
6. *Ibid.* p. 22.
7. see concepts in chapter 2.
8. Nehru, Jawaharlal, *The Discovery of India.* Oxford University Press; Centenary edition January 1, 1994. P. 426.
9. Nehru, Jawaharlal, *Nehru on Gandhi: A selection, arranged in the order of events, from the writings and speeches of Jawaharlal Nehru.* The John Day Company: New York. 1948. p. 36-37.
10. *Ibid.* p. 40-42.
11. *Ibid.* p. 92-93.
12. *Ibid.* p. 93.
13. *Ibid.* p. 94-96.
14. *Ibid.* p. 102-103.
15. *Ibid.* p. 138.
16. *Ibid.* p. 139-140.
17. *Ibid.* p. 144.

4

Post Gandhism — I

(Gandhism Travels to America, A Land where Gandhiji Never Set Foot On)

> Great as this man of God was in his life, he has been greater in his death, and I have no shadow of a doubt that by his death he has served the great cause as he served it throughout his life.[1]
>
> —*Pandit Nehru*

Gandhian philosophy or Gandhism or Gandhian ways did not perish with the body of Mohandas Karamchand Gandhi, known to the masses as Mahatma Gandhi. As eternal as his soul, Gandhism remained a proactive approach.

When freedom of India became the talk of media all around the globe, it also highlighted Gandhiji. And thus, travelled Gandhiji's non-violence philosophy.

Bayard Rustin, A Gandhian Apostle

> . . . Rustin brought the message and methods of Gandhi to the United States. He insinuated non-violence into the heart of the black freedom struggle. He presided over the transformation of direct action tactics from the cherished possession of a few initiates to its embrace by millions of Americans. He resurrected mass peaceful protest from the graveyard in which cold war anti-communism had buried it and made it once again a vibrant expression of citizen rights in a free society.
>
> Rustin was a visionary. He believed that violence could never

> bring justice that war could never bring peace. He stood by these convictions during the "good war" against Hitler, during the first decades of the cold war, and during the years of a spiralling nuclear arms race. Rustin was an internationalist long before globalization became a catchword in American life. He viewed nationalism as a destructive force in human affairs and conducted himself as if world citizenship already existed. He organized and led protests not only in the United States but across several continents as well.
>
> Rustin was smart. His associates recognized him as a master strategist of social change. He dedicated himself to figuring out how human beings, individually and collectively, could do more than simply go about the business of living. He studied the workings of insurgent movements around the globe so that he might better understand how permanently to alter powerful institutions and longstanding national policies.[2]

Bayard Rustin lived a low profile, nevertheless, he stood like a pillar of non-violence in the midst of extreme commotion and movements. Self-proclaimed Gandhian, Rustin developed Gandhian ways and lived Gandhism.

He innately understood one of Gandhi's message very well that the person or the community standing up for one's own rights must stand up itself/himself/herself. And this is exactly what Rustin did.

He advocated not Gandhi's ways or duplicated Gandhi's methods, Rustin pondered over the non-violence philosophy and its underlying fundamental basic ethics and principles, *Dharma*. At first he explored and understood Gandhism in Gandhiji's context. He then transported his philosophy to America and contextualized in an American way and the way he could lead the movement. A smart anthropologist.

Rustin was a devout Christian, so, he expounded on '*dharma*' that exists in Christianity. Majority of Black Americans were and are Christians.

Point to note here is that among critics, Nehru, who held Gandhiji to be an orthodox Hindu was wrong in his assumptions. Gandhiji simply identified with his roots and chose to spend his life in a place, India, where he thought he would be of most help. And he was right. However, Gandhiji's confrontational approach was not narrowed to India or Indians only.

> . . .Rustin was in the vanguard of this new confrontational approach that adapted Gandhian non-violence to attacking racism in United States.[3]

Gandhiji not only intrigued Indians and British but he was a regular topic of commentary and discussion in the black newspapers of USA.

People from the states came to observe Gandhiji in India. Experience certainly, surpasses knowledge by far. Gandhi's articulation of *Satyagraha* and infiltrating the American pacifist movement is another example of Americanizing Gandhism and Americans making Gandhism their own so that they can stand up for their rights in America in an American way.

Gandhian philosophy doesn't hand you the fish, instead, it teaches you to be able to fish for yourself standing on your very own two feet. At macro level, it may be referred to as 'self-sufficiency', a virtue innate to India and Indians.

> As early as 1919, W. E. B. Du Bois, who edited the NAACP magazine, *The Crisis*, was directing the attention of his readers towards India, telling them, "We are all one - we the Despised and Oppressed, the 'niggers' of England and America." (23 - Du Bois quoted in Kanpur, Raising Up a Prophet, p.11. The information in this and the following paragraphs on the relation of African Americans to Gandhi is drawn from Kanpur.) By the 1930s, as the Indian independence struggle escalated, Gandhi's way was a regular topic of commentary in black newspapers.
>
> . . .Some of Gandhi's disciples came to the United States with the explicit purpose of reaching into the black community with the message of *Satyagraha*. Some white American missionaries returned to the United States transformed by their encounter with Gandhi and India. They became tireless proponents of Gandhian non-violence and racial equality. Black leaders also went to India to observe and learn. In 1935, Howard Thurman, the dean of Rankin Chapel at Howard University, and Sue Bailey Thurman, on the national staff of the YWCA, spent several months there. Returning to the United States, they lectured widely on Gandhi's crusade, especially before black colleges, churches, and clubs. As a divinity student at Howard

> just a few years later, Farmer came under the influence of Thurman.
>
> Gandhi's articulation of *Satyagraha* also infiltrated the American pacifist movement, especially the religious wing represented by the FOR. Richard Gregg, an American Quaker who spent several years in India in the 1920s, published The Power of Non-violence in 1935. A detailed exposition not only of how Gandhi employed non-violence but also of the philosophy behind it, Gregg's book became an essential primer for Rustin and other young religious-minded pacifists.[4]

'Harlem Ashram' was such a glowing example and hard-devoted work of J. Holmes Smith, a Methodist missionary who spent nine years in India observing, participating, learning and experimenting with non-violence in anticipation to awaken the souls of 'Black African Americans' so that their will to stand for their justice will qualify them for equality.

Let's review this perspective with Gandhiji's logic. In order to apply non-violence philosophy, one's soul has to be awakened which implies one's adherence to truth, discipline and other ethics as mentioned in chapter 1.

Once the soul is awakened, it is apparent that truth commands justice and gets it.

> Gregg himself served on the FOR's national council and worked with the AFSC. Another influential book was *War Without Violence: A Study of Gandhi's Method and Its Accomplishments* (1939) as a protest against the British salt tax. His presence on the Morningside Heights campus, just a couple of blocks from the FOR's Broadway office, facilitated an active interchange with Rustin, Farmer, and other for staff. Finally, J. Holmes Smith, a Methodist missionary who spent nine years in India, returned to the United States in the late 1930s eagre to plant *Satyagraha* on North American soil. Serving on the FOR's national council, Smith established in 1940 the Harlem Ashram, an experiment interracial living and a launching pad for non-violent direct action campaigns. Farmer and other FOR staff lived there for varying periods of time; Rustin visited often. Activities ranged from a largely symbolic interracial trek from New York to Washington, D.C., in efforts

> to change employment practices at the YMCA, downtown department stores, and Manhattan restaurants.
>
> With Muste's encouragement, FOR staff intentionally injected Gandhian non-violence into the struggle for racial justice in the United States. . .. Rustin, meanwhile, had become FOR's "one-man non-violent army" through his single-handed exploits around the country.(24 - Quoted in Farmer, Lay Bare the Heart, p.110)[5]

Racial injustice is untruth and yes, "one-man non-violent army" is sufficient to suggest the exploits and thus awaken other souls in the process as done by Bayard Rustin.

These mere suggestions of exploits such as "stool-sitting technique" were eye-openers not to the oppressor only but also to the oppressed as the oppressed masses started to feel their power rising as they took it in their own hands to humanize themselves.

Here, we realize the process of soul awakening in terms of humanizing. The oppressed masses, who had either started believing in their own inferiority or just never questioned their inferiority, looked upon themselves as an equal world citizens worshipping the same supreme power as the rest of the world. 'Self-respect' was awakened. And with that awakened their 'duty' to their 'rights'.

> As Rustin moved about the country, word of this young Negro began to travel beyond the groups he met face to face. In Washington, D.C., Pauli Murray was a student at Howard University in the early 1940s when, she recalled, "nobody had ever really seriously studied non-violent direct action in terms of group participation. But there were people like Bayard Rustin, and James Farmer, who was [sic] doing that same thing that I was doing, and I was reading things about Bayard Rustin and he inspired me. . . And so I began to experiment with non-violence." With other Howard students, Murray began using the "stool-sitting technique" at restaurants in black neighbourhoods that served only whites. Emboldened by some successes, the students then turned their attention to downtown restaurants with the aid of the campus NAACP chapter.(30 - Pauli Murray Interview, CRDP.)
>
> While Core Chapters were serving as laboratory settings to test Gandhian techniques, an opportunity emerged within the

> black community to reach a much larger working-class constituency. At the end of 1942, A. Philip Randolph announced that his March on Washington Movement (MOWM) would convene a national conference to explore non-violent civil disobedience as a means of striking at Jim Crow. As Pauline Myers, one of his deputies, explained, "If the national conference adopts this method the Negro people will be called upon to boycott trains, street cars, buses, restaurants, waiting rooms, rest rooms, hotels, schools and institutions that have jim crow laws. . . The aim is to harness the flow of rising resentment and indignation on the part Negro Americans that has become intensified due to the war."(31 - E. Pauline Myers, "The March on Washington Movement and Non-Violent Civil Disobedience," APRP, Box 26.) Randolph's announcement electrified the Gandhian enthusiasts in the FOR. Muste told the staff it was "as epoch-making as the launching in 1906 of Gandhi's own campaign in South Africa." J. Holmes Smith, who ran the Harlem Ashram, saw it as a "sensational development." It portended, he thought, "thrilling opportunities" to spread Gandhian revolutionary resistance.(32 - FOR Executive Committee Minutes, 1/12/43 and 1/26/43, FORP, Box 3.[6]

Through the methodology of Gandhian revolutionary resistance, Black African Americans began to exercise their rights as world citizens dutifully and wilfully.

> "People tend to forget their duties, but remember their rights."
>
> — *Indira Gandhi, India, PM*

Thus, soul awakening that leads to the path of truth-seeking renders one with self-respect and performing duties without any expectation of reward as mentioned in *Gita* and by John Ruskin.

When Congress passed the Selective Service Act of 1940, it made provisions for conscientious objectors.[7] Rustin took to this as an opportunity to exercise his duty to reform the mass' rights from the inside.

> . . .The federal district court issued an indictment, and, on January 12, Rustin was arrested. The following month, he waived the right to a trial and pled guilty. The judge sentenced

> him to three years and gave him ten days to settle his affairs. Rustin spent ten days in the West Street jail. He quickly made his presence felt. Two days after his arrival, according to the meticulous files that prison administrators kept on him, he was "proving to be very troublesome. Came to the business office without authorization. Later, became obstinate when ordered to go to his cell." Soon Rustin was in solitary, having refused to accept segregated tables in the dining hall.(10 - Central File Chronological Record, 3/2/44m BPNA.)
>
> Troublesome was hardly the word to describe the relationship between Rustin and the Bureau of Prisons. The bureau classified him as one of the system's "notorious offenders," a designation he shared with Al Capone, the Chicago mobster serving time in Alcatraz. From the beginning, he alarmed administrators, including James Bennett, the director of the bureau in Washington, who found himself having to pay inordinate attention to this obdurate inmate who wilfully ignored prison rules, followed the dictates of his own conscience, and dared guards to tame him. ..[8]

It is interesting to note that his comparison with Al Capone. Al Capone, the Chicago mobster. Bayard Rustin, the social reformist. Though comparing Rustin and Capone will be like comparing apples and oranges, the similarity lies in their behaviour perceived by the mainstream system, a threat. I still think it ludicrous, however, this sentiment of ludicrousness may apply to the system in place at the moment. Rustin, the visionary, saw the light.

> A few days later, while still in quarantine, Rustin sent Hagerman a several-page memo on racial segregation in the prison and how to end it. He proposed a small experiment of placing some "well-trained Negroes" in roles that would provide "a tacit challenge to creative thinking" about race relations. Specifically, Rustin suggested that he be allowed to teach in the prison's education department a course on American history to white and black inmates alike. He wrapped this modest recommendation in a lengthy disquisition on the principles and practice of non-violence. As if instructing a deficient student, Rustin walked Hagerman through the range of possible responses to injustice, from violence, acceptance, and avoidance, to nonviolent resistance. To the warden of a

> prison in which the lines of power and authority were supposed to be unambiguous, Rustin's memo could only have appeared as a threat.(17 - BR to Hagerman, 3/30/44, BPNA)[9]

Where Rustin saw the light, the administration saw the threat. Nevertheless, Rustin was able to pull some ropes here and there; and he was able to reform the racial policies of prisons from within the prison walls using methods of Gandhiji.

> All in all, this latest trial by fire pleased Rustin. Not only did he and the other pacifists hold to their principles, but they also emerged with substantial moral capital. Huddleston's attack "placed us in a position," he informed Grotewohl, "where we could ask the administration to maintain a firm and progressive position" on racial policy within the prison.(24 - Grotewohl to BR, 5/5/44, BRP, Reel 20; Bronson Clark to Grotewohl, 5/28/44, and BR to Grotewohl, 5/5/44, BRP, Reel.I.)[10]
>
> . . .With Worthy, Rustin seized every opportunity to bend Randolph's ear about "new racial techniques," as Worthy put it in a letter, by which he meant the methods by Gandhi.[11]

Rustin's take on Pacifism and non-violence hand-in-hand is particularly interesting because it suggests that pacifism and non-violence are almost the same; this suggests the obvious adoption of non-violence philosophy by pacifist Christians.

> Rustin lectured almost continuously on pacifism and non-violence. He told audiences about the hardships faced by COs in the United States - the jail terms and the prison strikes by incarcerated pacifists during the war. Rustin quickly learnt that "the people in India actually do not have respect for Western pacifists," as he reported to Muste, "because they believe we are not people who have in any way made a sacrifice. . . They are amazed to learn of the things that we have endured." Commenting on the inspirational impact Rustin had on his listeners, one Indian pacifist wrote to Sayre: "How we need a man like him in our colleges just now?" (9 - BR to Sayre, Muste, Newton, and
>
> Bartlett, n.d., Sayre Papers, DG 117, Series A, Box 14, SCPC;

and Dick [Koithahin?] to Sayre, 12,26,48, BRP, Reel 2, India File.)[12]

. . .. When the Indian Parliament abolished untouchability in 1947, the Pittsburgh Courier declared that it "makes Lincoln's proclamation pale in significance by comparison. . . [India] has moved far out in front of the United States."(1 - Pittsburg *Courier,* 5/10/47, p.6) Repeatedly in the campaign against military segregation, Randolph had held up Gandhi and India as models to emulate. Now Rustin was to have a firsthand view of the Mahatma's legacy and bring the lessons back to the United States.[13]

Through his interactions and lectures, Rustin was able to bridge pacifism and non-violent. People in India believed that western pacifists had not made any sacrifices because of some of early Christian missionaries with their forceful and monetary incentive ways to convert Indians to Christianity. In an attempt to overcome the lurking social stigmas in the United States, Rustin took the first plunge to understand Mahatma's legacy in India and then apply it in America.

Bayard Rustin, The Internationalist

Now was the time to realize that pacifism and non-violence are quite similar. This also sheds light on how Gandhiji was a world citizen despite being a devout Hindu and how Bayard Rustin was also a world citizen despite being a devout Christian. In other words, one doesn't have to shed his identity, religion, language, etc. in order to become worldly. This is proved in practice by two outstanding individuals and great souls; however, otherwise romanticized by the armchair critics.

Although Rustin also criticized Gandhiji for being a nationalist, he himself, mainly remained marked for the black people's cause. Both of them were similar in their approach that the oppressed himself/herself has to stand up for his/her rights. Gandhiji stood up for India's freedom and spent the rest of his life in uplifting the masses of India. Rustin was a black African American Pacifist and he, using the same methodology as that of Gandhiji in conjunction with pacifism, helped immensely with the social-racial-injustices inflicted on Black African Americans.

In other words, the non-violence philosophy can, in essence, be applied in any circumstances.

> . . . Nehru talked to Rustin about his intention to keep India out of the grip of the cold war. "India can save world peace," he thought, "by helping in the construction of a third entity" that sided with neither East or West. The Prime Minister reminisced how Gandhi "refused to show up at the celebration of Independence because he was heart broken by so much violence." But Nehru also told Rustin that "the tap root of Gandhi's motivation was nationalism" and that, since Independence, the centrality of nationalism in the struggle to remove the British had become clear.(11 - notes of Sayre about BR's India visit, and BR to Ewbank, 3/28/49, in FORP, Series D, Box 1) . . . Without underestimating Gandhi's achievement, Rustin emphasized that nationalism had corrupted the movement from the beginning and, without the continuing influence of Gandhi, the non-violent movement in India was in deep trouble. . . . It was non-violent in its means, but essentially violent in its ends, which was nationalism." Nonviolence in India was a matter of "expediency.. embraced because they had no guns."(12 - National Council Meeting Minutes, 5/19-21/49, Rustin report on India, copy in FORP, Series D, Box 1)
>
> . . . Lester told Muste that Rustin was "getting into the very centre of power here and perhaps no one else could work so effectively with Nehru against militarism." Wherever he had gone in the country, "things started happening about pacifism," she reported. "Now is the moment in India," she concluded, and Rustin's continuing presence was "utterly necessary."(13 - Koithahin to Sayre, 12/26/48, BRP, Reel 2, India File, Rustin Papers, and Lester to Muste, 12/26/48, FORP, Series D, Box 1.)[14]

Just the fact that both Nehru and Rustin critiqued Gandhiji in different light shows their own inherent perspectives with their very own determination and respective goals. On contrary, Gandhiji refrained from criticizing anyone else because he was the doer. If he came across something bad, he didn't give in to his temptations, instead he walked on. If he came across something good, he embraced it without question. In reality, Gandhiji was very pragmatic.

The reason why he didn't attend the celebration of India's Independence because, considering himself a man of the masses, he did not want to disappoint anyone who might have disagreed with such an idea or the methodology of it. It is an open book that Independence of India came with too much effort and just as much controversy. The violence of masses, which he was able to tranquil for the longest time, might have erupted if he had chosen to celebrate along with politicians and certain schemers. Gandhiji simply stuck to his original role of a doer as explained in *Gita* and as chosen by his free choice. He complied with the responsibility he had taken on. Other point to think about is that, if Gandhiji was an utter nationalist then he certainly would have joined the celebration of India's Independence. Nehru misunderstood Gandhiji and misinformed Rustin about Gandhiji. This might have been a factor in Rustin's perspective of Gandhiji being a nationalist.

Rustin was also wrong in his conclusion about non-violence doctrine being applied in India due to lack of guns. It is probably true that India lacked guns to fight the British. But it is also true that Gandhian non-violence quieted enormous riots erupting with or without guns.

The essence of non-violence overlooked by Rustin was that Gandhiji not only wanted to free India from the clutches of a colonial empire, but also from any other cancerous stigmas so that the 'free India' will be able to sustain its freedom from within and outside evil forces and India be a secular country.

As Gandhiji had reformed the thinking in India and in Indian thought, Rustin, to a great extent, influenced the outlook of pacifists.

> Rustin unquestionably touched the hearts of many who heard him speak. He shaped the outlook of the young pacifists-in-training with whom he worked intensely. Yet whereas he could point to successes in the work for racial justice, it would be hard to claim that his activities in these years shifted by even a degree the trajectory of the cold war. Certainly that was how Roy Finch, a veteran of CPS camp during World War II and part of the inner circle at the War Resisters League, saw it. "What we thought was going to happen," he reminisced, "was that there would be an inevitable swing towards peace after

> the war. The fact is that the war never ended, and we never expected that. . . I think people just had the feeling that all you could do was sort of symbolic things. . . The peace movement was helpless. Absolutely helpless. I don't think it did a thing."(35 - Finch Interview, JDI.)
>
> . . . The pacifist had to accept this. "Basic social change," he wrote to a student who had heard him speak, "involves a vast deal of physical violence. The pacifist is not a man who is afraid of violence nor in a sense opposed to using violence, but he must be prepared to accept it as a part of social change." As Jesus did, the pacifist had to "take it unto himself" and recognize that "you cannot take a stand for truth and justice without. . .causing some suffering."(37 - BR to Beverly White, 5/3/50, FORP, Series D, Sox 1, Folder 5.)[15]

Rustin prepared the pacifists to stand up to any physical pain in the cause for truth and justice. The end result being the same, both Rustin and Gandhiji not only brought about social reform but also set a stage for a continued path of social reform of eradicating social and racial inequality. The work had just begun. The souls were just starting to be awakened. *Dharma* was ready to be invoked.

Africa Awakes to Gandhism

> In the middle of the Korean War, an opportunity arose to escape the deadeningly conservative atmosphere of the McCarthy era. For more than a year, Rustin had been planning a trip to Oxford in the summer of 1952 as a delegate to the World Conference of Friends. As the time for his departure approached, Rustin's attention, as well as that of Houser, Bill Sutherland, and other close associates, turned towards events in Africa. In South Africa, the African National Congress had launched a series of demonstrations against apartheid. Manilal, one of Gandhi's sons, informed Muste that the campaign bore all the markings of a non-violent resistance movement. "Father's spirit seems to be watching over and guiding them," he wrote with pleasure.(39 - FOR Executive Committee Minutes, 9/15/52, FORP, Box 4.) In West Africa, resistance to colonialism was gathering. Especially in Nigeria and the Gold Coast, political movements led by Nnamdi Azikiwe and Kwame Nkrumah seemed to be developing along lines pioneered by Gandhi's fight against British imperial rule.

> Rustin and Houser began hatching a plan that melded their commitments to peace, racial justice, and non-violence. What if they reoriented their work towards support for African decolonization? How could Americans, themselves a product of a revolutionary war against an empire, not respond with empathy? Might opposition to Western colonialism be a way to preach non-violence, win support for campaigns against racial injustice, and avoid being tarred with the brush of cold war anti-communism? And so Rustin's trip to Oxford became instead part of a larger expedition to Africa to meet independence leaders and see how American pacifists might support the freedom struggles there. [16]

Bayard Rustin was a product of a different political-social arena than Gandhiji. Still applying Gandhiji's methods Rustin saw through the politics of part and present colonialism and set his plans in motion to include the freedom of many African countries. Bayard Rustin used his movement and methods of Pacifism and non-violence to meet similar ends, such as freedom struggles, as Gandhiji had done. India since time immemorial is considered a sub-continent and Gandhiji was the man for that. As for Rustin, he turned towards his own people whether they be in America or in African countries.

Rustin Leads African Nationalism

Rustin's travels and works did give rise to African nationalism and were intertwined with politics.

> . . . His weeks in the Gold Coast and Nigeria, his meetings with Kwame Nkrumah and Nnamdi Azikiwe who were leading their countries' independence movements, his contacts with Africans on the streets of Lagos and Accra-together they touched something deep. The six seeks in Africa unlocked passions both political and personal. (1 - Quoted in Goldman, The death and Life of Malcolm X, p. 173; Rustin, "Negro America: Inspiration to Africa," WRLP, Series B, Box 18.)
>
> Much of the excitement of his travels stemmed from politics. "Africa is afire," he wrote to colleagues at home. "From the Mediterranean to the Cape of Good Hope, every imaginable form of resistance is being used to break 300 years of

> . . . European domination. Everywhere, African nationalism is rising."(2 - Rustin Memo, October 20, 1952, FORP, Series D, Box1, "Writings and Speeches.") The Gandhian in him thrilled to the commitment to non-violence that he found among some of the independence leaders, but he also saw that its roots were not deep. Hatred of the colonizers was rife, and in Rustin's view, it boded poorly for the future. Without a liberation strategy anchored in the goodwill of non-violence, "Africa may reach independence but miss freedom. A change of exploiting leadership from white men to black men is not worth the struggle," he wrote. "But just such a limited change is highly possible unless a revolutionary method is used that can recognize evil everywhere it exists—even in the African community — and accepts good everywhere it exists—even from the European settlers." Looking at African politics through the eyes of a Gandhian apostle, Rustin saw non-violence as "perhaps the only method that can keep Africa from turning further toward communism and black nationalism. . . It is the only power method ultimately capable of drawing a clear line between progressives and reactionary elements."(3—Unless otherwise noted, the quotations in this and the following paragraphs come from a series of essays by Rustin, typescript in WRLP, Series B, Box 18, "Rustin: 1962" Folder. The titles are "Non-Violent Revolution in the Gold Coast"; "Revolution Reaches Africa"; "Nkrumah, Man of Ghana and God"; "Negro America; Inspiration to Africa"; and "Nnamdi Azikiwe: Nehru of Nigeria.")[17]

Regardless of Rustin's influence on the rising African nationalism, it became apparent that the non-violence philosophy is the only such methodology that can not only free Africans but also promise them independence void of exploitation whether that be by the colonized or the colonizers.

> . . . Rustin observed that "I have never met two men more alike than Zik and Nehru. Each is fiery and sensitive. Each has a world view. Each has the love of his people. Each is willing to expend all for the people." Most of all, Rustin reflected poignantly, "each respects the ideals of Gandhi and each is inwardly sorry he cannot see clearly to follow him all the way." Nkrumah also made a powerful impression.
>
> Rustin was struck by "his organizational genius, his animal

> magnetism, his honesty and his judgement of the temper of the people." Rustin rated him "not just a nationalist. He has a burning revolutionary spirit. . . He is an internationalist." Attuned to the power of music, Rustin noticed that wherever he went in the Gold Coast, he heard improvised tunes about Nkrumah.[18]

Rustin's observation that Zik and Nehru are similar in their world view and respect ideals of Gandhiji but do not see Gandhiji's ways clearly confirms Gandhiji's willingness to stay out of politics because his ways which are for social reform primarily may not necessarily be the ways of political reforms or the ruling political institutions. This flattery between the social and political reform was felt not only in India but also among people of African descent.

It is interesting to note that Rustin's criticism of Gandhiji being a nationalist, pointing towards himself. In other words, non-violence is, thus far, a political and just approach to root out evil.

According to Rustin, Nkrumah is a revolutionary internationalist, however, it is interesting to note that Nkrumah was appreciated much amongst mainly African descent people whether they be in Nigeria or Gold Coast. It is simply a matter of binding culture. For Gandhiji the culture was binding amongst Indian descent people in South-Africa and India whereas for Nkrumah the culture was binding amongst African descent people in Nigeria and on Gold Coast.

Bayard Rustin Mentors Martin Luther King Jr.

At last Rustin came in touch with Martin Luther King Jr. and became his mentor till King's assassination. Despite his coaching from literature about non-violence, King learnt a lot from Rustin not only in terms of speech but a way of life of a non-violent individual.

> Over the next few days, Rustin and King conferred several times, initiating a long and complex relationship that would last until King's assassination. Rustin became teacher to a pupil whose fame would soon outstrip his mentor's. . . . "The fact of the matter is," Rustin recalled, "when I got to Montgomery, Dr. King had very limited notions about how a non-violent

protest should be carried out," There were guns lying all about King's house, and Rustin often recounted a humorous incident with himself and Bill Worthy. As Worthy, who had followed Rustin to Montgomery by a couple of days, prepared to sit on one of the chairs in King's living room, Rustin called out to him, "Bill, wait, wait. Couple of guns in that chair. You don't want to shoot yourself."(14 - Rustin Interview, CUOHC.)

To Rustin, efforts either by King's followers or by historians to present King as a fully developed Gandhian at the start of the boycott were a disservice to a man. "He had not been prepared for [the job] either tactically, strategically, or in his understanding of non-violence," Rustin emphatically told an interviewer. "The glorious thing is that he came to a profoundly deep understanding of non-violence through the struggle itself, and through reading and discussions which he had in the process of carrying on the protest, not that, in some way, college professors who had read Gandhi had prepared him in advance. This is just a hoax." Arriving in Montgomery a week after Rustin, Glenn Smiley confirmed Rustin's evaluation. About Gandhian non-violence, Smiley insisted, King "knew nothing." (15 - Rustin Interview, CUOHC; Smiley Interview, JDI)

Rustin's Gandhian credentials were impeccable. He had what King most immediately needed: extensive experience in non-violent protest. But Rustin also had something more - years of serious meditation about how the philosophy, strategy, and tactics of non-violence were of a piece and how together they might fashion a transformative revolutionary movement. Rustin particularly remembered one long discussion that he characterized as "very important" in which he shared with King his reflections on the Indian independence movement. His trip to India, he told the young Montgomery leader, taught him that the mass of Indians who followed Gandhi were not philosophically wedded to non-violence. But they were willing to take it up as a tactic because they believed it would be the most effective way to end British rule. That makes it all the more critical, Rustin impressed upon King, for the leadership to "be dedicated to it in principle, to keep those who believe in it as a tactic operating correctly. . . If, in the flow and heat of battle," he told King, "a leader's house is bombed, and he shoots back, that is an encouragement to his followers to pick up guns. If, on the other hand, he has no guns around him, and they all know it, they will rise to the non-violent occasion of a situation." From the start, Rustin communicated to King not

> only the efficacy and moral value of non-violence, but the special responsibility of leaders to model it fully."(16 - Rustin Interview, CUOHC)[19]
>
> But there was something more, something that made Rustin the perfect mentor for King at this stage in the young minister's career. Rustin had melted Quaker, Gandhian, and Marxist persuasions in ways that were unusual, if not unique. His Christian faith, which ran deep, kept his moral outlook clear and in focus; the Quaker inflection to his faith, with its pacifist tradition and non-conforming stance, made social activism his gospel. In Gandhi's biography, Rustin had found a practice that breathed life into his values, promising their realization in this world, not just in the next. And from Marxism, Rustin drew the conviction that the pursuit of peace and racial justice was inextricably bound to a quest for economic justice. Putting these influences together made Rustin a radical strategist able to combine vision, values, and program.[20]

The genius, Rustin, put an unthinkable mix together and brew a potion of contemporary peaceful revolution for his era.

Gandhiji, the pioneer who had set on this path of non-violence had actually discarded Marxism because it entailed violence through conflict of classes. Nonetheless, there is a glimpse of Marxism in John Ruskin's views of love of labour. Pacifism and Quaker also have striking similarities in Hinduism and in Indian thought. In other words, Rustin, the genius of America, did manage to African-Americanize Gandhian non-violence to work for the African-Americans in America and in African countries.

So, it is right on to say that Rustin had years of serious meditation about how the philosophy, strategy, and tactics of non-violence were of a piece and how together they might fashion a transformative revolutionary movement. He had the perfect recipe.

> . . . Rustin was as responsible as anyone else for the insinuation of non-violence into the very heart of what became the most powerful social movement in twentieth-century America.[21]

Rustin was a national Anthropologist of his time without him or anyone else knowing about it. He didn't merely acted upon his ideas but his ideas were well meditated upon and were a by-product of a mix of participation and observation. As he had found necessary to visit India in 1949, as King's mentor, Rustin thought it wise for King to visit the land where this non-violent revolution came to such heights.

> From the time King's work in Montgomery became an international story, a chorus of voices pressed King to travel to Gandhi's homeland. Certainly Rustin encouraged the idea, as did many others in the American pacifist community. Unlike in 1949, when Rustin's presence in India provoked concerned cables from American diplomats, by the late 1950s, King's stature in the movement for racial equality made him an ideal American emissary to an Asian nation unaligned in the cold war. Chester Bowles, a former American ambassador to India, wrote to King excitedly about the prospect of a visit. "Nothing would spread more goodwill for America than a visit here by someone who has tried to apply Gandhi's principles in the United States," Bowles wrote King. "As you know, there is nothing that hurts our relations with Asians more, or undermines America's prestige more than our lingering racial discrimination."(35 - Bowles to MLK, 1/28/59, copy in BRP, Reel 3, MLK Folder.)
>
> The AFSC contributed much of the financing for King's 1959 visit, planned an itinerary to coincide with King's wishes, and provided King and his wife, Coretta, with a guide. It saw the trip as an opportunity to deepen King's connection to an international community dedicated to non-violence. Yet the venture proved disappointing and frustrating to the AFSC. Jim Bristol, the staffer in India who devoted weeks of time to it, was disturbed because, "this whole trip is being thought of in terms of the *return* to U.S.A. and what will make an impact and produce an effect there." He described the kings as "going through India wearing *BLINDERS*." By the times they left, all Bristol could say was that "the whole experience has been a nightmare."(36 - Bristol to Dee ___m 2/25/59; Bristol to Corinne Johnson, 3/10/59; Johnson to Bristol, 3/26/59, all in AFSCA, "Foreign Service 1959, International Centers Programme.")[22]

Done all in good faith but failed at recourse. Bayard Rustin and Gandhiji were natural Anthropologists with innate 'emic' and 'etic' approach. But this was not the case with King Jr.

Why the visit failed was because there was no attempt to get to know the 'other' culture and or to understand its ways by 'participating' in it. If at all, it was thought of only in terms of 'return' to USA and its impact in USA, where there was no experience on which to expound upon/from.

Comparing the approach of Rustin and King, it is apparent that Rustin observed and participated in Indian ways and then Americanized them whereas King (could be due to his advising team) didn't observe and participate in Indian ways and thought, and so he could not apply Indian ways in America.

Non-Violence to Achieve Justice and Peace

> As 1960 ended, Rustin prepared for a trip to India. The War Resisters International was holding its tenth triennial conference there, the first time it would meet outside Britain. The American delegation was small. Besides Rustin, it included Willoughby, the head of CNVA, and Jeannette Rankin, the first woman to serve in the U.S. Congress and the only American elected official to have voted against participation in both world wars. Friends like Bill Sutherland and Michael Scott attended; altogether, sixty-four countries were represented.
>
> The choice of India was both symbolic and strategic. Travelling to the country that had been home to Gandhi honoured the memory of a man who was a heroic figure to everyone in attendance. The Indian locale also implicitly . . . the stance of many Western pacifists. The War Resisters had formed in Britain in the wake of First World War as an uncompromising voice against the staggering carnage of the conflict. Over the years, its members had tended overwhelmingly to emphasize a pure and simple opposition to warfare. But Gandhi used non-violence differently. He directed it against colonialism. His target was injustice — the injustice of one nation exploiting and impoverising another and robbing it of dignity and autonomy. In 1960, the continuing struggle to end European imperial rule preoccupied the delegates from Asia and Africa. It was at least as vital as opposition to nuclear weaponry, which absorbed Western pacifists. Moreover, the site of the conference was at Gandhigram, a training center and retreat founded by G. Ramachandran, a disciple of Gandhi. Gandhigram served

> as a base for the chief manifestation of non-violence since Independence — the reconstruction of village life along egalitarian economic and social lines.

Gandhiji, a mystery to Pandit Nehru, prior to the Independence of India, unravelled as the free India demanded ways to implement democracy. In Rustin's own words, Nehru now started to see the light into the mysterious Gandhiji. He saw coercion in democratic ways of the west and felt to concede with the complete non-violence philosophy of Gandhiji.

> . . . But the Gandhian movement in India had demurred, claiming that in a democracy where citizens could express their will through electoral channels, direct action campaigns were coercive. Instead, they argued, all their efforts should go towards building a "Gandhian society" that would willingly reject armed violence. But, Rustin reported, "before long it became apparent that many Indians feel that use of direct action 'embarrasses Pandit Nehru, our old friend and leader.'"(7 - WRL *News*, NO. 106 (March/April 1961), pp.2-3.). . .
>
> Rustin spoke about his concept of social dislocation, of the need for pacifists to create what he called "non-violent confusion" in society. He urged upon his listeners the broadest conception of their mission. "I have learnt in my work the greatest lesson of all." he told them. "Whether the problems be that of colour or caste, man can be unjust to man, American to American, India to India. The problem is rooted in man's ability to be unjust, and therefore, can only be approached basically if we are opposed to all injustice." By the time the conference ended, his words had carried the day as conference participants endorsed — for the first time in the WRI's history— the use of non-violence "to achieve social justice as well as peace."(9 - *The War Resister*, First Quarter, 1961; Rustin, "Non-Violent Direct Action for Racial Integration," *WRL News*, No. 106 (March/April 1961), pp.2-3.)
>
> When the conference ended, Rustin and Willoughby stayed in India for several more days. They travelled together to Calcutta to meet Vinoba Bhave, the inheritor of Gandhi's mantle and the instigator of the campaigns to redistribute land voluntarily in India's rural villages. For several days, the two Americans travelled with Bhave through the countryside, trekking from

> village to village. At one point, the two men made an excursion to an ancient Buddhist center. "It was in ruins," Willoughby recalled. "We went out there very late at night or early in the morning, bright moonlight. Here's this vast pile of ruins. And you know Bayard was a collector. 'Look at these things!' Bayard was just wild to see this whole field. There were hundreds of feet of ruins of these old Buddhist temples. You could just push around in them."(10 - Willoughby Interview, JDI.)[23]

In 1960, when Rustin visited India again, he stuck to his previous ways of taking in and learning from the other culture and seeking ways of applying it to the problems he faced in his community, society, nation etc.

What is interesting is that with time Rustin gradually approached similar conclusion as those drawn by Gandhiji, for example – the use of non-violence 'to achieve social justice as well as peace': most importantly, achieve all social justice and peace.

Gandhiji has also started with pinpointing one injustice, that of colonialism, and then he moved to remove any and all injustices from the whole of India. Rustin also reached similar conclusion of that of opposing all injustices in his movement.

People's Non-Violent Army Becomes International Peace Brigade

Furthermore, the concept of 'World Peace Brigade' reemerged as suggested by Gandhiji in 1948 but the idea withered with his sudden assassination.

> During the months in London, Rustin also devoted himself to another pacifist project just then taking shape. In 1948, immediately after Indian Independence, Gandhi had proposed the creation of a people's non-violent army, recruited from all over the world, to intervene in places where war threatened. Gandhi's assassination had forestalled any efforts at implementation, but the idea continued to circulate through pacifist networks. At the Gandhigram conference, Ramachandran had broached the concept in his welcoming

> address. "Nationalism and what are called national states have become largely menaces to the human spirit and to human society." he told the international assemblage. He challenged them to "go beyond patriotism and nationalism. We must declare that we can accept no frontiers of any national state. . . Humanity is one and we are citizens of one world." Jayaprakash Narayan, another Indian delegate followed with a specific call for a "World Peace Brigade." Rustin drew warm applause when he called for the use of direct action as "an integral part of any such international brigade."(22 - "Tenth Triennial Conference Report," *The War Resister*, First Quarter, 1961.)
>
> . . . "Discussion of a World Peace Brigade has plagued us since Second World War and the idea should either be implemented or forgotten," he told his fellow pacifists.(23 - "Tenth Triennial Conference Report," *The War Resister*, First Quarter, 1961; and Rustin, "Report from India," *WRL News*, No. 106 (March/ April 1961), pp. 2-3.)
>
> Despite his brusque tone, Rustin wanted it to work. Its boldness appealed to him. More than the moral witness of a transcontinental walk, it promised direct intervention to forestall mass violence. . . . He was particularly intrigued by the role a peace brigade might play in Africa. . .[24]

"International Peace Brigade" was at last formed in 1962 meant to take on the power of imperial interests and cold war alliances. Imperial interests and cold war alliances are western by-products and concepts. Since Gandhiji wanted to keep India a par of cold war effects, he had simply theorized it as People's Non-violent Army. With Rustin's efforts in the era of post-Gandhism People's non-violent army took the form of International Peace Brigade.

> Through the fall of 1961, pacifists in Europe, Asia, Africa, and North America engaged in a spirited, often contentious, debate about just what this peace brigade should do. . ..
>
> Right after Christmas, Rustin, Muste, and Bob Gilmore travelled to Lebanon for a conference to launch the brigade. Held at a Quaker high school in a suburb of Beirut, the meeting had impressive sponsorship: independence leaders like Julius Nyerere of Tanganyika and Kaunda of Zambia; philosophers like Martin Buber of Israel and Bertrand Russell of Britain; Martin Niemoller of Germany, a theologian whom the Nazis

> had imprisoned for seven years; Danilo Dolci, the Italian radical often described as "the Gandhi of Sicily." Assembling in the unheated school, which was closed for the holidays, and suffering through unusually cold weather, the delegates from thirteen countries endorsed recruitment of a multinational nonviolent army. "Nothing could be more fantastic," remarked Gilmore, as he contemplated what it meant to take on the power of imperial interests and cold war alliances.(26 - Barbara Deming, "International Peace Brigade," *The Nation*, 4/7/62, pp. 303-306.) Specifically, the conference decided to approve a plan to assist African independence movements.[25]

Bayard Rustin Debates Malcolm X

Many rallies were conducted and many gatherings took place. Despite the resistance from the USA government administration, Rustin never faltered on his path to fight for racial justice. He also debated on many occasions with Malcolm X, his equal in charisma and a powerful public speaker. Despite their contrary approaches to social justice, in specific, racial injustices in USA, both had one similarity of never giving into violence themselves. The major difference between them was that Rustin preached what he lived, i.e. non-violence through and through verbal and physical, whereas Malcolm X spoke of rhetorical militancy though he never took to arms himself.

> . . . With the involvement of WSP, the protests that WRL and CNVA sponsored began to grow. In March 1962, 3000 opponents of nuclear testing gathered in New York's Times Square, and after the rally, some of them engaged in an impromptu sit-down. The next month, over 5000 participated in the annual Easter Peace Walk, which Rustin addressed outside the United Nations. In October, in the midst of the Cuban missile crisis, Rustin coordinated a quickly planned demonstration in front of the UN. The rally brought together more than 10,000 marchers, the largest peace demonstration in New York since the cold war began.
>
> . . . In 1962, Martin Luther King lent his effort to an ongoing disegregation campaign in Albany, Georgia. The local police chief made so many arrests that the jails of neighbouring counties had to house the demonstrators. The tempo of civil rights activities was certainly rising, but there were few

institutional gains to show for it. The movement seemed up against immovable obstacles.

One of the largest obstacles was the Kennedy administration itself. For all the idealistic rhetoric that emanated from the White House, President Kennedy and his brother Robert, the attorney general, were reluctant to act on behalf of racial justice. . . . Kennedy's approach was that "there was going to be plenty of time to fight the battle of civil rights legislation." Meanwhile, "his desire to do first thing first" meant that racial justice remained relatively low on his list of priorities.(35 - Farmer, King, and White Interviews, JFKL.)

Rustin kept as best he could some connection to the fight for racial justice. A mesmerizing speaker, he was a great crowd pleaser and remained much in demand. During 1961 and 1962, he engaged in a series of public debates - in New York, Chicago, and Washington, D.C. — with Malcolm X, a charismatic leader in the Nation of Islam, or Black Muslims as they were popularly called, espoused racial separatism and advocated armed self-defense. . . . His advocacy of mass action and strategic non-violence when sit-ins and freedom rides were capturing the public's imagination more than matched the rhetorical militancy of Malcolm X. And Rustin could taunt his opponent on the weakness of the Nation's political strategy. "The Black Muslims have put forth, as you ought to know, no concrete programme except speaking on 125th street," he said during one of their debates.(36 - Transcript of Rustin / Malcolm X Debate, video copy in author's possession.)[26]

If only Malcolm X had furthered his thinking and struck a balance between his speeches and his way of life; his way of life was non-violent just like that of Bayard Rustin.

Rustin Jailed for Obeying Non-Violence

Rustin's true test of non-violence came with Johnson signing the Voting Rights Act followed by deployment of about 200,000 military personnel to fight in Vietnam. Obeying non-violence throughly, he chose prison in the place of army.

Early in August, Rustin travelled to Washington to witness Johnson's signing of the Voting Rights Act. He stood in the

> room where a century earlier, Lincoln had signed into law a bill freeing some of the South's slaves. Rustin received one of the pens Johnson used in the ceremony. By the time he arrived home, federal registrars were already heading South to enter African Americans on the voting rolls. The Justice Department suspended literacy tests across the region and filed suit in court to challenge the constitutionality of state poll taxes.
>
> As Rustin watched Johnson sign the Voting Rights Act, some of his former colleagues in the peace movement stood mutely outside the White House. Muste, David Dellinger, and Staughton Lynd, along with Bob Moses of SNCC, had gathered in Washington on the twentieth anniversary of the bombing of Hiroshima. Several hundred others joined them in a silent vigil in front of the White House as a protest against the president's policies in Southeast Asia: over the preceding month, Johnson had ordered the deployment of almost 200,000 military personnel to fight in the war that was raging in Vietnam. To the pacifists outside the White House, Rustin's presence inside symbolized a parting of the ways.[27]

A believer in social dislocation and the doer of social reform indeed remained elusive in his death as he did in his life. He achieved what he did not only with his persistence but also because what he persisted on was just. And following the ethics and principles as laid out by Gandhiji, one will reach that state of being just and fearlessness, so very apparent in the life of Bayard Rustin. His Quaker ways and pacifism belief set him on this path of being internationalist or a visionary with a world view.

> Despite the tributes and the many front-page obituaries, Rustin remained as elusive in death as he had in life. The accounts of his life were rife with inaccuracies. He was said to have met Gandhi; his diction was attributed to West Indian roots or a London education. Even the attempts to characterize his politics stumbled. The *New York Times* attempted to trace a career trajectory that moved from radical to conservative, but Rustin's own words spoke out defiantly. "I know that I have changed," the obituary recorded him as saying. "But the changes have been in response to the objective conditions." As if finally to acknowledge the rebelliousness that had characterized his life, the editor chose this as the featured quote:

> "I believe in social dislocation and creative trouble."(30 - See obituaries of Rustin in the *New York Times*, Washington *Post*, Los Angeles *Times*, and Chicago *Defender*, all 8/25/87, See also New York *Amsterdam News*, 8/29/87; *New Republic*, 9/28/87; *Guardian*, 9/9/87; and *New Leader*, 9/7/87.)
>
> In the last years of his life, Rustin was fond of repeating a statement that he attributed to A. Philip Randolph: "The struggle must be continuous, for freedom is never a final act." A few months before Rustin died, a young admirer asked how he kept hopeful in dismally conservative times. "I have learned a very significant message from the Jewish prophets," Rustin replied. "They taught that God does not require us to achieve any of the good tasks that humanity must pursue. What the gods require of us is that we not stop trying."(31 - "Human Rights in the World: Speech to the Anti-Defamation League," 10/25/80, BRP, Reel 18; Rustin Interview, Bowman.)[28]

Bayard Rustin, who was a great non-violent soul, a pacifist, succeeded to a greater degree in bringing about social reform, social justice and peace in the United States of America and abroad among other African countries. And he never stopped trying.

Rustin, the genius revolutionary, used peaceful means to reach peaceful ends. Therefore, peace must be a non-violent journey.

Notes

1. Nehru, Jawaharlal. *Nehru on Gandhi: A selection, arranged in the order of events, from the writings and speeches of Jawaharlal Nehru*. The John Day Company: New York. 1948. p. 132
2. D'Emilio, John. lost prophet: *The Life and Times of Bayard Rustin.* The University of Chicago Press, Chicago: 2003. p. 1-2.
3. *Ibid.* p. 50.
4. *Ibid.* p. 52.
5. *Ibid.* p. 52-53.
6. *Ibid.* p. 56.
7. *Ibid.* p. 72.
8. *Ibid.* p. 75-77.
9. *Ibid.* p. 80-81
10. *Ibid.* p. 85.
11. *Ibid.* p. 187.
12. *Ibid.* p.166.

13. *Ibid.* p. 161.
14. *Ibid.* p. 166.
15. *Ibid.* p. 181-182.
16. *Ibid.* p. 183.
17. *Ibid.* p. 184-185.
18. *Ibid.* p. 185-186.
19. *Ibid.* p. 230-231.
20. *Ibid.* p.236.
21. *Ibid.* p. 237.
22. *Ibid.* p. 268.
23. *Ibid.* p. 304-307.
24. *Ibid.* p. 314-315.
25. *Ibid.* p. 316.
26. *Ibid.* p. 322-324.
27. *Ibid.* p. 407.
28. *Ibid.* p. 493.

5

Post-Gandhism - II

(Rosa Parks, an Innate Gandhian)

The ethics guided by Gandhiji, and implied and confirmed in the walk of life of Bayard Rustin, are not unusual at all. There are many individuals among us who instigate and emanate such ideals. One of them is Rosa Louise Parks who helped immensely to change the course of racial history in USA by simply doing what she felt right and that as a world citizen. Her courage came from her self-realization and her strong family background. A symbol of freedom for the world, Rosa Parks' quiet courage, dignity and determination knows no bounds.

Interestingly, Rosa Parks' ideals in life are very similar to that of Gandhiji. She also shed fear as taught to her by her grandfather. She put her trust in god and sought him as her strength. This also draws a parallel to Gandhiji's beliefs then and his followers' beliefs now.

> Rosa Louise Parks is nationally recognized as the mother of the modern-day civil rights movement in America. By refusing to surrender her seat to a white male passenger on Montgomery, Alabama, bus on December 1, 1955, she set in motion a chain of events. . . courageous act changed America and redirected the course of history.

When Rosa Parks refused to move from her seat only to give her seat to a white male, she set an example for all of her people and many of whom followed her ways. The simple act changed the course of history in United States. As this 'stool-sitting' technique, as referred to by Bayard Rustin started taking place everywhere, this also set in motion a powerful revolution that was peaceful and based on truth with a world-outlook challenging the existing conventional racial injustices and the extreme brutality of Ku Klux Klan. Remaining active in the civil rights movement, Rosa and her husband opened ways to the youth. A similarity is reflected of Rosa Parks and Gandhiji as both in-tuned themselves with their life-partners and became stronger in their chosen path of life.

> Mr. and Mrs. Parks moved to Detroit in 1957, and she remained active in the civil rights movement: travelling, speaking, and participating in peaceful demonstrations. From 1965 to 1988 Rosa worked in the office of Congressman John Conyers of Michigan. Her husband died in 1977, and in 1987 she began the Rosa and Raymond Parks Institute for Self-Development. Its purpose is to motivate and direct youth to achieve their highest potential. Rosa sees the energy of young people as a real force for change. It is among her most treasured themes as she speaks at schools, colleges, and national organizations around the country.
>
> An example of quiet courage, dignity, and determination, Rosa Parks is a symbol of freedom for the world.[1]

Though aware of prevalent violence and crime in the society, Rosa remains hopeful with the determination and dedication that her work continues of that of motivating and directing the youth to achieve their highest potential.

> As a child, I learned from the *Bible* to trust in God and not be afraid. I have always felt comforted by reading the Psalms, especially Psalms 23 and 27. My grandfather also influenced me to not be afraid. A very proud man, he was never fearful—especially when it came to defending his home and family. Back in those days, fear was something very real for black people. There was so much hatred toward blacks—especially from white supremacy groups, like the Ku Klux Klan(KKK).
>
> I remember one day when the KKK came near our house after many incidents of hate crimes against nearby blacks. My grandfather never seemed afraid. At night he would sit with

> his shotgun and say that he did not know how long he would last, but if they came breaking in our house, he was going to get the first one who came through the door. He never looked for trouble, but he believed in defending his home.
>
> I saw and heard so much as a child growing up with hate and injustice against black people. I learned to put my trust in God and to seek Him as my strength. Long ago I set my mind to be a free person and not to give in to fear. I always felt that it was my right to defend myself if I could.
>
> I have learned over the years that when one's mind is made up, this diminishes fear; knowing what must be done does away with fear. When I sat down on the bus the day I was arrested, I was thinking of going home. I had made up my mind quickly about what it was that I had to do, what I felt was right to do. I did not think of being physically tired or fearful. After so many years of oppression and being a victim of the mistreatment that my people had suffered, not giving up my seat—and whatever I had to face after not giving it up—was not important. I did not feel any fear at sitting in the seat I was sitting in. All I felt was tired. Tired of being pushed around. Tired of seeing the bad treatment and disrespect of children, women, and men just because of the colour of their skin. Tired of the Jim Crow laws. Tired of being oppressed. I was just plain tired.
>
> I felt the Lord would give me the strength to endure whatever I had to face. God did away with all my fear.[2]

Just like Indians, African decent people are also notoriously religious with grassroot spirituality, which, when realized, awakens the soul and invokes *dharma*. At that moment of realization of truth/ love, there is 'No Fear'. This falls precisely under the definition of a Gandhian *Satyagrahi*. Similar paths of people, oceans apart, provides credibility to universality of non-violence philosophy and its worldly outlook.

> It was time for someone to stand up—or in my case, sit down. I refused to move.
>
> We blacks are not a fearful or divided as people may think. I cannot let myself be so afraid that I am unable to move around freely and express myself. If I do, then I am undoing the gains we have made in the civil rights movement. Love, not fear, must be our guide.

> In these days, many people are feeling a different type of fear that is hard to break free of. There are so many new things to be afraid of that were not as common in the earlier days. We should not let fear overcome us. We must remain strong. Violence and crime seem so much more prevalent. It is easy to say that we have come a long way, but we still have a long way to go. Many of our children are going astray. But I still remain hopeful.[3]

Love without fear lends not only strength but also keeps hope. After she set an example by not moving from her seat, she was reprimanded and let go from her job. She could have played her race card as many opportunists do. However, she remained strong with her conviction and determination of what is just. This is similar to Gandhism that states that a *Satyagrahi* must accept the consequences of aftermath of a *Satyagraha*. Rosa Parks accepted the non-pleasant consequences and she remained hopeful, still, i.e. remained on her path of *Satyagraha*.

> A month after the boycott began, I lost my twenty-five-dollar-a-week job when the new defunct Montgomery Fair department store closed its tailor shop. I was given no indication from the store that my boycott activities were the reason I lost my job. People always wanted to say it was because of my involvement in the boycott.[4]

Self-respect is on the uppermost of Rosa's list of ethics because that is where it starts. One will feel the will to live just if one respects oneself. Another significant pattern to notice is that Rosa's ethics are passed on from her elders in the family, not by preaching but by exemplifying.

> If you want to be respected for your actions, then your behaviour must be above reproach. I learned from my grandmother and mother that one should always respect oneself and live right. This is how you gain the respect of others. If our lives demonstrate that we are peaceful, humble, and trusted, this is recognized by others. If our lives demonstrate something else, that will be noticed too. [5]

Self-respect gains respect of others. Rosa Parks' role models were her very own family members – mother, grand-father and later her husband, Raymond Parks. Note that all of Rosa's family role models were fearless.

> One thing that really impressed me about [Raymond] Parks was that he refused to be intimidated by white people—unlike many blacks, who figured they had no choice but to stay under "Mr. Charlie's" heel. ("Mr. Charlie" was our name for white men in general.) Parks would have none of it, and he became active in the NAACP and in civil rights issues.
>
> Parks worked courageously for the release of the Scottsboro Boys, a group of nine young black men who were wrongly accused of raping two white women in 1931. They were found guilty and condemned to die for a crime they did not commit. They did not die, thanks to the efforts of many. Anyone who supported them had to meet in secret. To do anything openly for this cause could mean death. And yet Parks, along with the NAACP, fearlessly pursued justice for these men. That is why I later decided to name my legacy after Raymond so that people would know how devoted he was to civil rights and the uplifting of blacks.[6]

Rosa Parks was just as influenced by her husband and her family as by the outsiders such as Martin Luther King Jr. and Malcolm X. Despite her strong background, even she doubted non-violence in the beginning. However, her adherence to truth and justice pulled her through.

> Martin Luther King Jr. set a profound example for me in day-to-day living. He was such a young man—just twenty-six year old—when I first met him at the beginning of the bus boycott. I was forty-two.
>
> I'll always remember the way Dr. King would respond to violence. He would use the same words that Jesus said on the cross: "Father, forgive them, for they know not what they do." Brutality was to be received with love, he would say. Though I knew we needed to strive for non-violence, when I saw the brutal treatment some of us got, I had trouble believing it was always the best thing to do. . . .

> During the civil rights movement, another young man came forth to help black people fight the unjust treatment they were receiving. His name was Malcolm X. He was twenty-seven years old. When I look back, this strong-willed man reminded me somewhat of my grandfather. He was full of conviction and pride in his race. The last time I saw him, he was speaking in Detroit, and he signed a programme for me.
>
> I admired the way he had changed his position from one of distrust toward whites to one of tolerance and building self-respect among blacks. His ideas were different than what many of us heard publicly, but his strong conviction of self-determination and pride energized blacks in economic development. The way he stood up and voiced himself showed that he was a man to be respected.[7]

At first, Rosa Parks distrusted non-violence which might have attracted her momentarily toward Malcolm X's rhetorical militancy. It is Malcolm's change of position from one of 'distrust toward whites' to one of 'tolerance and building self-respect among blacks' that reinstated her faith in 'non-violence'.

> During the civil rights movement, we were troubled by hatred. We would pray a lot. One thing we used to keep us going was the moving words of certain hymns, many of which had been passed down from the slave days. They gave us a sense of togetherness without people. Singing gave us the feeling that—with God's help—we could overcome whatever we were facing.
>
> One of my favourite hymns is "Woke Up This Morning with My Mind Stayed on Jesus." We would sing, "Woke Up This Morning with My Mind on Freedom." Another is "I Am Bound for the Promised Land." Often we would substitute the word "freedom" for a key word of the hymn.[8]

Sometimes, the little things by themselves seem irrelevant, but when put in some cohesive order, they seem to come alive, which is the case with singing hymns and holding debates on issues.

Gandhiji had also emphasized on spirituality which in practice led to prayers, moments of silence, education, singing of spiritual hymns, etc.

"Gandhiji used to observe silence for one day in every week.

—*Jawaharlal Nehru*[9]

This quiet path of non-violence enrages the indomitable will for quiet strength – the strength to bear and strength to continue.

> Many ask whether I am discouraged in the struggle for justice, peace, and harmony. My answer has always been no. People will need help whenever and wherever they are oppressed. As long as any effort is being made to help others, I will not allow myself to be discouraged. I prefer to have a positive attitude and focus on positive ideals. If you let yourself become discouraged, then you do not have much to look forward to.[10]

When Rosa Parks says "I will not allow myself. . .", she is exercising her free choice. One chooses with her/his own will to embark on this non-violence journey just the same way as Gandhiji had.

Here we also find a parallel of ways of Rosa Parks to that of Gandhiji which render Nehru and Bayard Rustin's (amongst many others) criticism of Gandhiji, fruitless.

Rosa Parks' strength mainly came from the church just as Gandhiji's strength has been critiqued to be solely enclosed within Hinduism and at times within India or within Indian Thought.

Gandhiji was very clear about his ways of non-violence when he mentioned that another person from another community or nation or religion will have to make it his/her own philosophy first by applying his/her own *dharma* to it and then that oppressor will have to stand-up for himself/herself.

A perfect example of that is to be seen in the lives of Bayard Rustin, Martin Luther King Jr., Rosa Parks, Nelson Mandela, Natives of North-America etc.

> My strength has always come from the church. I have always gained strength from thinking about the *Bible* and from the faith of my family. Church has always been a place where we can turn to God for rest and encouragement. It lifts the spirit

> and helps us to go on. Wherever, I travel, I try to attend a church service.
>
> Perhaps my only "secret" is my attitude toward life. Because I have such high ideals, I feel strongly when they are violated in the world around me. I do not like to see people treated in a way I would not want to be treated. Whenever, I see this happening, I do everything in my power to help the cause.
>
> People all over the world need help. There is still famine in Somalia, war in the Middle East, the ruins of apartheid in South Africa, and many other places of conflict. As long as the civilized world allows inhuman treatment to be inflicted upon any people, then our freedom is threatened as well.[11]

It is clear that Rosa's strength comes from the church. In general, one's strength comes from the religion one believes in or one has grown accustomed to as growing up.

Regardless, her 'secret' is her attitude toward life. And her attitude toward life is her freedom of choice. She simply treats others the way she wants to be treated herself, simultaneously she expects and stands up for the ways she ought to be treated by others. Be the change you want to see in others.

Gandhiji had felt the same. Being a barrister, he was allowed a lot more freedom than an average Indian, which he refused to practise until and unless all Indians were treated the same by British Raj.[12]

Rosa takes a proactive approach of mirror ideals to prepare children for the future. Gandhiji also used to say, preach what you do, not what you say. Similarly, Rosa suggests that "Rather than be so hard on them, we should instead act an example for them to follow."

> We must teach children to prepare for the future — how to set goals for their lives and for their careers. We must do more to inspire, train, and motivate them. They need effective role models to help them develop strength of character. They should be taught to understand the difference between knowledge, feeling, and behaviour. Rather than be so hard on them, we should instead act an example for them to follow. Here are seven key areas we can use:
>
> 1. Treating all youth with love and respect, setting good

examples for them, supporting social behaviour and correcting negative behaviour.

2. Helping all young people to know one another as persons and to respect and care about one another,
3. Teaching values by using the rich content of history, literature, and the *Bible*.
4. Showing young people how to develop the ability to work hard and to do the best that they can do.
5. Encouraging youth to work together so they can see the value of cooperating with others for a common good.
6. Guiding young people in experiences that show them how to solve problems without conflict and force.
7. Providing opportunities for youth to perform school, home, and community services.

> What message would I have for young people today—of any race? Work hard, do not be discouraged, and in everything you do, try to make our country—and the world—a better place for us all. You are among my treasured friends and this country's most treasured possessions. You are our future. I see your energy as a real force for change. But you must know who you are, where you are, and where you have been so that you will know where you are going. Once you know this, then you will be on the pathway to freedom.
>
> Do not forget to exercise self-control, nurture your spiritual life, and remain health-conscious. Stay away from drugs and alcohol, or else your mind and body will not be free. And remember, no matter what the circumstances are, it is best to pursue behaviour that is above reproach, because then you will be respected for your actions.[13]

In essence Rosa Parks and Gandhiji share the same spirit. Their ethics and principles are almost the same. For example, exercising self-control is equivalent to stern discipline; and nurturing spiritual life is equivalent to faith and trust in God which lends strength to adhere to truth (Truth is God, Gandhiji had maintained.) and to a state of fearlessness.

Just like Gandhiji and Bayard Rustin, Rosa Parks uses non-violence to bring about justice, peace and harmony. Peaceful means provide peaceful ends, and therefore, peace must be a non-violent journey.

Notes

1. Parks, Rosa with Reed, Gregory J. *Quiet Strength: The Faith, the Hope, and the Heart of a Woman Who Changed a Nation*. Zondervan Publishing House, Grand Rapids, Michigan: 1994. p. 11-14.
2. *Ibid.* p. 16-17.
3. *Ibid.* p. 18.
4. *Ibid.* p. 26-27.
5. *Ibid.* p. 42.
6. *Ibid.* p. 46.
7. *Ibid.* p. 49-51.
8. *Ibid.* p. 58-59.
9. Nehru, Jawaharlal. *Nehru on Gandhi: A selection, arranged in the order of events, from the writings and speeches of Jawaharlal Nehru*. The John Day Company, New York: 1948. p.143
10. Parks, Rosa with Reed, Gregory J. *Quiet Strength: The Faith, the Hope, and the Heart of a Woman Who Changed a Nation*. Zondervan Publishing House, Grand Rapids, Michigan: 1994. p. 70.
11. *Ibid.* p. 70-71.
12. Attenborough, Richard. Director, Gandhi.(movie) 1982.
13. Parks, Rosa with Reed, Gregory J. *Quiet Strength: The Faith, the Hope, and the Heart of a Woman Who Changed a Nation*. Zondervan Publishing House, Grand Rapids, Michigan: 1994. p. 82-84.

6

Post-Gandhism – III

(Oka Blockades - A Motion Toward Satyagraha)

A Kanehsatake Mohawk Attempt of Satyagraha

Triggered by the land dispute and fuelled by the shooting of a police officer, the native blockades initiated by Kanehsatake Mohawks were similar to a *Satyagraha*. July 11th, 2010 marked 20th anniversary of the Oka crisis.

Torn between the non-violent traditionalists elected band councils and the militant hard-liners, the 78 days standoff saw a mix of both.

At first sight, if Gandhiji was to assess this crisis, he might have mourned the death of one police officer to the extent of calling off the blockade. However, on the other hand, he might have insisted on extending the blockade with no arms whatsoever.

In a way, the 78 days blockade saw no violence after that one incident.

The blockade by the natives was a way to '*agrah*' (protest) for '*satya*' (truth). What had rightfully belonged to the First Nations should have remained so.

There were more than 2500 people from across the continent. "Spirit was with us," said a spiritual leader from Mexico[1].

Oka crisis became a turning point in the History of North-America. It not only brought them together but instilled a broader conscience amongst First Nations of their integrity and rights. Their organizational skills of sending messages from band to band all across Americas were phenomenal.

> "It made me feel better to be native. I felt stronger," said Barney McLeod, an Ojibwa sculptor living in Vancouver, who quit his construction job in Toronto during the crisis and drove all night to deliver canned food to Kahnawake.
>
> "A lot of people felt sorry for themselves for being native. But after Oka, native people became prouder and stronger."[2]

The '*agrah*' to keep the land of their ancestors, the Kanehsatake Mohawks as First Nations people of North America united to command their rights.

> "I look at Oka as a victory, a victory for native rights," said Kenneth Deer, editor of the Mohawk newspaper, The Eastern Door, "In the end, the government had to listen to us."[3]

The '*agrah*' that united First Nations people of North America to command their rights also united them in their values and beliefs. The Oka crisis ignited their soul awakening and they realized their *dharma*. Though caught in the indecisive moments of supporting militant hard-liners over non-violent traditionalists elected band councils, realization of *dharma* came to their aid to lessen violence.

Confronted with the loss of their ancestral land to a commercial uplift for the elite, the natives felt the loss through their complex system of mutual respect.

"We are here to defend democracy against people who don't understand democracy. . . We have done nothing wrong. They are trying to break our spirit."[4]

> According to Native North American traditions, everything that the creator makes, whether animate or not, has a spirit. Therefore, all things are related and all things are sacred. Relationships between humans, Mother Earth, other creatures and the ancestors are well defined. . . People are therefore

> expected to respect the earth. . . Humans must also respect their living kin, and must provide and care for each other in order to survive.
>
> , . . Every traditional rite and ceremony celebrates the spirit that unites all things on earth and reaffirms the sacred relationships.[5]

As mentioned above, the Native North American tradition also attempts to "uphold" or "sustain" the positive order to things: the nation, the community, the family and ultimately, even the universe. The concept of 'Human and Nature' is omnipresent amongst the natives of America just much amongst the Indians from India.

Therefore, it is a rightful deduction that religion, duty and righteousness are all, that are included within the concept of *dharma*, are also part of the Native North American tradition.

Emanating from *dharma* is duty and spirituality, leading to soul-awakening which leads to the path of non-violence, and thus, peace.

At this point, it will not be wrong to state that non-violence is a holistic, all encompassing and a fundamental step-stool to grass-root spirituality that leads the peaceful journey that ends in peace. Peaceful means provide peaceful ends, and therefore, peace must be a non-violent journey.

Notes

1. Obomsawin, Alanis. Director, *Kanehsatake - 270 Years of Resistance (Oka Mohawk Uprising).* (movie) 1993.
2. *Crisis inspired Many Native People, History.* First Nations drum.
3. *Ibid.*
4. Obomsawin, Alanis. Director, *Kanehsatake - 270 Years of Resistance (Oka Mohawk Uprising).* (movie) 1993
5. Zimmerman, Larry J. *Native North America.* Little Brown and Company, Toronto: 1996. p. 74.

7

Searching for Peace where the ends Define the Means

"They say, 'means are, after all, means. I would say, 'means are, after all, everything: As the means so the end. . ."

— *Mahatma Gandhi*[1]

"One day we must come to see that peace is not merely a distant goal that we seek, but that it is a means by which we arrive at that goal. We must pursue peaceful ends through peaceful means."

—*Martin Luther King, Jr.* (1929-1968)

"There is no way to peace, peace is the way."

— *A. J. Muste* (1885-1967)

"Peace is every step."

—*Thich Nhat Hahn*

Gandhiji and his likes such as Martin Luther King Jr., A. J. Muste who held much influence on Bayard Rustin and who shaped Rustin's path, and Thich Nhat Hahn (a Buddhist monk, teacher, author, poet and a peace activist) — all of whom are peace messiahs — agreed on peaceful means. They all strove for peace, achieved it and passed it on.

It is interesting to note that Thich Nhat Hahn joined a Zen monastery at the age of 16, studied Buddhism as a novice, and was fully ordained as a monk in 1949. The title Thich is used by all Vietnamese monks and nuns, meaning that they are part of the Shakya clan as from Shakyamuni Buddha. Buddha had actually revivified *dharma* at the time when the orthodoxy of the institution of religion was starting to pollute and Indians were being led astray from their grass-root spirituality. A much deeper philosophy and enlightenment of *dharma* is to be found in Buddhism.

There is a trickle down effect in the message of Thich Nhat Hahn of peace being every step. This suggests peace must be present and consistent from micro level (individual level) to macro level (world level) and *vice versa.*

This trickle down effect of peace from macro level (world peace) to micro level (individual peace) was also documented more than 20 centuries ago.

If there is to be peace in the world,
There must be peace in the nations.

If there is to be peace in the nations,
There must be peace in the cities.

If there is to be peace in the cities,
There must be peace between neighbours.

If there is to be peace between neighbours,
There must be peace in the home.

If there is to be peace in the home,
There must be peace in the heart.

— *Lao Tzu* (570 - 490 B.C.)

The notion of peace has always existed. The methodology of peace as means has been documented since time immemorial. So, why have we not been able to achieve peace?

Nobel peace prize is awarded to promote peace. Still, why is there no peace?

The answer is simple. We do not want to be the change we want to see in the world.

Mahatma Gandhi had expounded on this point and exemplified it by living his life in a peaceful manner, in a non-violent manner.

> "Be the change you want to see in the world."
>
> — *Mahatma Gandhi*

Needless to say that the above is an individual approach. Nevertheless, it is not impossible to attempt it at a larger scale.

According to Lao Tzu, peace in the world will follow from peace in the heart. This bottom up approach is the grassroot approach devised by Gandhi through awakening the soul.

As the soul is awakened to *Dharma* — which is that upholds or sustains the positive order of things: the nation, the community, the family and ultimately even the universe — peace in the world is the obvious conclusion.

Subsequent to peace is freedom. When the soul is awakened to *dharma*, soul is liberated to perform one's duty to sustain positive order without expectation of reward. Expectation arises greed and ego without which one is free to perform his/her duty to his/her fullest capability as suggested via *karmayoga* in *Bhagwad Gita*.

> "You can't separate peace from freedom because no one can be at peace unless he has his freedom."
>
> —Malcolm X (1925 – 1965)

The aggressive personality humble trait, Malcolm X, was quite far-sighted to associate peace with personal freedom of being, i.e. self-identity leading to self-respect. When you see yourself as you are with all your faults and strengths and you accept yourself as you are with all your faults and strengths, peace starts to settle in your heart - first step to soul awakening. An awakened soul attempts to uphold via co-operation and co-existence not only with other souls, but also with nature and other forms of life.

This is by no means Utopia. On the contrary, this is Gandhian

Utopia. This peaceful approach has been attempted by many from time to time on the ladder of success.

Let's explore some global current examples of means to achieve peace. It has been established thus far, that peace as end-only doesn't instill peace; therefore, we will explore mainly the means, deployed globally, to achieve peace.

Peace Keeping Forces

> Can forces actually work towards keeping peace?
>
> *No.*
>
> Can aggression exert calm?
>
> *No.*
>
> Can a war be fought to bring about peace?
>
> *No.*
>
> And just why not?
>
> Is it because the military forces aren't coercive enough to keep peace?
>
> Or aggression is not strong enough to exert calm?
>
> Or violence can actually breed non-violence?
>
> *Impossible.*
>
> Or a war is not waged with all its rage and bloodshed to instill fear to bring about oppression, sometimes interpreted as peace simply because oppression can be silent.

To all these multifaceted questions, there is only one answer - Peace is. Peace is alive. Peace is dynamic. Peace is not static in a sense that it is idling somewhere where we can go and take it. Peace does not prevail by uttering the word peace..All the outcries of peace do not bring about peace. Chanting the word peace does not help to attain peace. Registering Associations, organizations and the like about peace is just a methodology to follow through in order to apply for funding from government and commercial conglomerates and or collect charity funds, the funds which may help the needy or may generate income for the one collecting; however, that still doesn't guarantee peace.

We are all trying to cover up the symptoms of what and where peace is not. And we call that working toward peace. We write volumes on the bloodshed, wrong doings, exploitation and extortion. And we call that literature on peace. Artists drum up concoctions of melancholic melodies and rhythms. And this is considered peace music.

All this will be for peace if done with peace at heart and peace in intent as one walks along the journey of peace. Only anything done in a peaceful manner is peace. In other words, only peace as means will bring peace as an end that will maintain and sustain.

Therefore, peace keeping forces, which suggest use of force, are not capable of providing peaceful means, consequently no peaceful end, and thus, no peace.

Education

> "All we are saying is give peace a chance."
>
> —*John Lennon (1940–1980)*

Why not? Why can we not teach peace. If arts can be taught, performing arts can be taught, psychology can be taught, philosophy can be taught, meditation can be taught, war can be taught, terrorism can be taught - then most certainly peace can also be taught. Peace must be taught.

> "Since wars begin in the minds of men, it is in the minds of men that the defences of peace must be constructed."
>
> — *UNESCO Constitution*

The best way to construct the defences of peace is by sharing peace ideologies, passing them on, and most of all peace must become that pedestal of *dharma* to sustain the positive order of things; the nation, the community, the family and ultimately even the universe.

For example, social science courses are full of conflicts and draw experiences from war, riots, invasions etc. Learning about conflicts due to war, riots, invasions etc. instills an individual with violence, vengeance and hatred. Until and unless the individual realizes the fundamental necessity of peaceful solutions, one most likely may not seek peace. The result is most apparent among undergraduate students. In fact, the undergraduate students are manipulated to attend in massive numbers, simply because they add to the number crunching of man-power, in holding various protests and stand-offs. Students are 'manipulated' mainly and easily because they are an easy target to be fed selective information. This gives rise to radical thinking.

On the contrary, if the students are primarily taught about peace ideologies and secondarily taught to seek each and every solution using peaceful means, the progress will be gradual and development will be sustainable; unlike the virtual progress and development of 21st century.

The progress today is virtual because it is based mainly on GDP which is solely a number crunching game of money rotating in the market. More money rotates in the market, higher the GDP is. More money rotating/consuming structures are there, more money is rotated. This generates the need to build more money rotating/consuming structures. The 21st century has saturated the existing or conventional money rotating structures and now it is encroaching on sub-dividing the larger money-rotating structures. Consumer saturated markets, such as North America and Europe are now once again seeking markets abroad in highly populated countries like India and China because there exists the manpower to buffer the consumer need. The question is for how long?

Whether in the East or West or North or South, everyone is aware that this trend of virtual economy is at its wits end..

Even the attempts to recycle it by reteaching the same social, economical and political theories are lax. Without much a due, a new approach is needed. For the new approach to be most effective, it will have to come from within, with a conviction. In other words, a social reform is on demand.

A social reform is easier said than done. Nonetheless, if we follow the Gandhian philosophy of non-violence, that stands on a single pillar of 'Truth', a social reform will take place.

Adhering to truth, will put in motion a gradual slow-down of virtual progress and development. It has always been and it still is possible to gradually slow-down and lessen the speed of virtual economy and virtual development. The only reason why it hasn't been done is because the agenda, thus far, of ruling politicians and economists has been to build the virtual structures. Further, the agenda has been handed down to the educational institutions to reproduce the curriculum in the manner that will reinforce the structures.

There is nothing wring with having structures but we have lost the equilibrium.

In today's age, the structures are hardly feeding and protecting the people, instead people are going out of their ways to maintain the structures. Again, the healthy balance is lost. And the way to regain the balance is through a gradual slow-down and then a gradual restructuring of virtual economy and development.

Education that reinforces the structures may also participate in lessening and restructuring of them and simultaneously maintain a balance.

The ultimate challenge lies not in teaching peace or non-violence but how to teach it. Perhaps it should be passed on by exemplifying. Or perhaps both, i.e. praxis, a theory of Gandhian philosophy of non-violence. And these are the means and so the end.

> "Gandhi rejected the idea the injustice should, or even could, be fought against "by any means necessary" — if you use violent, coercive, unjust means, whatever ends you produce will necessarily embed that injustice. To those who preached violence and called non-violent actionists cowards, he replied: "I do believe that, where there is only a choice between cowardice and violence, I would advise violence. . . I would rather have India resort to arms in order to defend her honour than that she should, in a cowardly manner, become or remain a helpless witness to her own dishonour. . . But I believe that non-violence is infinitely superior to violence, forgiveness is more manly than punishment."[2]

Non-violence is certainly infinitely superior to violence and forgiveness follows from non-violence subsequently. However, forgiveness does not mean forget because if we forget, the history will most likely repeat as it is already happening. Regardless, forgiveness (without forgetting) is more manly than punishment. This is the ultimate challenge for *Education,* to teach the truth and to forgive from the heart without forgetting, via using peaceful methods and means in order for peace to prevail; a peaceful end through peaceful means. Therefore, peace must be a non-violent journey.

Notes

1. Prabhu, R. K. and Rao, U. R. (editors) "The Gospel of Sarvodaya". *The Mind of Mahatma Gandhi.* (revised edition) Ahemadabad, India: 1967.
2 Prabhu, R. K. and Rao, U. R. (editors) "Between Cowardice and Violence". *The Mind of Mahatma Gandhi.* (revised edition) Ahemadabad, India: 1967.

8

All Encompassing Non-Violence

> "Just as one must learn the art of killing in the training for violence, so one must learn the art of dying in the training for non-violence. Violence does not mean emancipation from fear, but discovering the means of combating the cause of fear. Non-violence, on the other hand, has no cause for fear."
>
> —*Mohandas Karamchand Gandhi*

Non-violence is perceived today as a philosophy that the scholars hold discourses on, like it is just another one of those ideas.

Non-violence is mocked by the commoners who are enveloped with the culture of violence tamed by a few leaders who head the communal riots along with religious riots — which are for the benefit of a few leaders, nevertheless, they affect a lot of common people; so when the common people experience nothing but violence in the name of religion and/or community solidarity etc. - Yes, they mock non-violence.

Non-violence is a weapon used by the strong to retain one's perception of strength and to keep the feeble in feeble's place. Satirically pondering – why the Political Superpowers, after achieving all the means for destruction, have simultaneously opted for Saving the World from Nuclear Destruction?

Non-violence is used as an ultimate shield when all other forms of violence and communication fail. At the brink of failure of communication, Gandhi had led the Salt March. This multi-faceted phenomenon/philosophy of non-violence has been apparent in history time after time.

Nevertheless, Mohandas Karamchand Gandhi, brought this philosophy to surface by reaching deep down to his cultural and heritage roots during his stay in South Africa. However, Mahatma Gandhi neither presented non-violence as a philosophy nor held theoretical discourses on it. He demonstrated the praxis of non-violence, i.e. he did not teach non-violence rather he exemplified non-violence; and yet he taught non-violence to the world. According to Gandhiji — 'You must be the change you want to see in the world.'

So, how and why Gandhiji lived non-violence? How and why he succeeded in living non-violence? Let's reflect on the sociology of Gandhi's life. He grew up in quite a traditional family, i.e. with Hindu or at a larger scale Eastern ideals, beliefs and values. He learnt law abroad, i.e. he acquired the skills of western critical thinking and reasoning and he learnt how to penetrate the mechanism of 'western' policies and procedures.

According to Audre Lourde, an American author, . . . The structures cannot be broken from within because they are built to protect themselves.

Now let us consider the dilemma of Gandhiji. He was a professional lawyer and a good one on top of that. He had the skills to combat the governing bodies of the world within their domains. He entered their world but found himself to be an alien or from the other side of the fence. He wanted to make the changes from within. But his credits didn't matter. His skills didn't matter. He was an Indian but his education had taught him the ways of non-Indians. He was a non-Indian but he had the longing for his cultural heritage and he was in no way not-proud of it. In a nutshell, he was a simple clear-hearted well-educated Indian entering the real world. So, he chose the best in both of his worlds and made it work. Thus, we have Gandhian Attire of Non-Violence.

> "I became disgusted with the profession. As lawyers the counsels on both sides were bound to rake up points of law in support of their clients; the winning party never recovered all the costs; I felt it was my duty to befriend both parties and bring them together. I realized that the true function of a lawyer was to unite parties driven asunder," mentioned Gandhiji[1].

The very basics of Western and Eastern philosophical fundamentals which were brought together in the Gandhian approach of Non-violence were the following.

Western political philosophy which starts with Hobbes stating that human is evil by nature and needs to be controlled, thus, is the need for political systems entwined with the management of policies and procedures.

Eastern philosophy as a whole has always maintained that the human is peaceful by nature, which is developed from the concept of human as a spirit, thus, there is the concept of inner peace or peace emanating from within.

As Gandhiji attempted to blend the two schools of thought together, eastern and western, he developed his doctrines with intricate logic and spirituality; in addition he kept in mind the differences of the East and West freedom struggles as well in order to determine what will work in India. Regardless, in the end, his doctrines of *Satyagraha* and non-violent non-co-operation made an impression worldwide.

A primary example is: the two terms, '*Satyagraha*' and 'passive resistance' are used synonymously; however, as one seeks a deeper understanding of '*satyagraha*', the term 'passive resistance' ceases to be synonymous. According to Gandhiji, in 'passive resistance', there is admittance of violence as in the case of suffragettes and violence is universally acknowledged to be a weapon of the weak; moreover, there is no emphasis on adherence to truth under all circumstances. Therefore, 'passive resistance' is different from *satyagraha* in the following ways.

1. *Satyagraha* is a weapon of the strong whereas passive resistance is acknowledged to be a weapon of the weak.
2. *Satyagraha* admits of no violence under any circumstance whatsoever whereas there is admittance of violence in passive resistance.
3. *Satyagraha* always insists upon truth whereas passive resistance doesn't necessarily command adherence to truth.

A *Satyagrahi* may obey the laws of society intelligently and of his own free will. Fasting is another potent weapon of the *Satyagrahi* but it is of no use without a faith in God; soul awakening. A *Satyagrahi* must never mere imitate another *Satyagrahi*, unless one feels from the depth of one's soul. Thus, is the reason for rare *satyagrahis*.

Gandhiji also recommended to every man and woman to learn the art of self-defence. Not the self-defence apparent in the West where every adult man enlists for army training for a definite period. The training for *Satyagrahi* is not physical, rather it is mental training for all, irrespective of age or sex. Due to the nature of the mental training, there can be no compulsion or force, thus, no violence.

A secondary example is: Gandhian movement of non-violent non-co-operation does not have much in common with the historical struggles for freedom in the West. Gandhian movement of non-violent non-co-operation is not based on hatred or brutal force, and therefore, does not aim at destroying the tyrant. It is actually based on the concept of co-existence mentioned in chapter 1.

Gandhian non-violent non-co-operation movement is targeted first and foremost at self-purification so as to convert the tyrant. Non-co-operation is one of the main weapons in the armoury of *Satyagraha* to be used as means to secure the co-operation of the opponent consistently with truth and justice. Non-violence praxis seeks to neutralize the hostility and not the hostile party. A *Satyagrahi's* objective is to transform or purify the relationship with the opponent through non-violent non-co-operation movement.

Gandhian Anarchy

According to Gandhiji, civil disobedience or non-violent, non-co-operation is the inherent right of a citizen; civil disobedience is never followed by anarchy, however, criminal disobedience may lead to anarchy since criminal disobedience has elements of violence and every state puts down criminal disobedience by force or violence.

In blending the concepts and shaping his doctrines, Gandhiji applied '*dharma*' i.e. basic principles of eastern philosophy which also happen to be the basic principles of 'Hinduism' or 'Indian Thought' and came up with the fine-tuned form of *Satyagraha* to combat the 'at that time' current policies and procedures hindering the freedom of India.

Satyagraha

Literally it means *Satya* (truth) with *Agraha* (firmness) or, unwavering search for the Truth. Gandhiji emphasized that *Satyagraha* is the most potent method of ensuring an endurable Peace. He further mentioned that (i) Truth is God; (ii) Non-violence is Love in Action; and Peace, the result of enduring conflict resolution, is the Fruit of *Satyagraha*.

Gandhiji practised two forms of *Satyagraha* – civil disobedience and non-co-operation. Gandhiji ruled out direct coercion, such as trying to physically block someone; hostile language; destroying property; and not even any secrecy was permitted. All these were ruled out because any of them would undercut the empathy and trust which Gandhiji was trying to build, and it would hinder that "change of heart", i.e. a social reform. His followers had to take the face beating, imprisonment, confiscation of their property cheerfully hoping that this willing suffering will bring about that social reform that will cause a "change of heart."

The non-co-operation had dynamics of its own which was based not on appeals but on the power of the people themselves. Converting the opponent or even molding the public opinion was not part of the agenda. Non-co-operation was dynamic – which implied 'No fear."

Coercion is effective only as long as it is feared. For ex: prisons are feared, tear gas is feared, torture is feared etc. What if people, outright, declare that they are not afraid to go to prison, they don't fear tear gas and they don't fear torture? What then? When there is no fear, coercion fails.

'No Fear' is a process that follows from approaching non-violence as creed vs. policy.

Non-Violence or Ahimsa as a Creed and as a Policy

According to Gandhiji: "Laws to be laws admit of no exceptions" and non-violence is the law of our being.

Gandhiji preferred persuasion to coercion just as the Greeks did i.e. persuasion to be a mark of the civilized. Gandhiji had even laid down five simple axioms of this based on his argument that a creed has to be all-pervasive and cannot pertain only to certain activities and ignore others, while a policy cannot have the strength of "a life-force." The five axioms are:

1. "Non-violence implies a complete self-purification as is humanly possible" – i.e. a stern discipline while maintaining ethics and principles outlined in chapter 1.
2. "Man for man the strength of non-violence is in exact proportion to the ability, not the will, of the non-violent person to inflict violence" — i.e. a non-violence person with determination to remain non-violent is stronger that the person who inflicts violence.
3. "Non-violence is without exception superior to violence, i.e. the power at the disposal of a non-violent person is always greater than he would have if he was violent" – i.e. non-violence is a weapon for the strong only.
4. "There is no such thing as defeat in non-violence. The end of violence is surest defeat." Non-violence means seek to negotiate and co-exist; therefore, nobody loses and everybody wins; whereas use of violence necessarily creates the hierarchy of winners and losers; someone always loses.
5. "The ultimate end of non-violence is surest victory – if such a term may be used of non-violence. In reality, where there is no sense of defeat, there is no sense of victory" – i.e. the votary of *ahimsa* never aims at defeating anyone but merely at achieving a desirable result.

Let's also reflect on the critics of non-violence. If the idea of non-violence or *ahimsa* was or is, in fact, wholly impossible then inevitably the humans would have destroyed themselves by now. However, our presence in the present dynamics is a witness that humans are not destroyed, though it seems to be heading in that direction from time to time. So, what is it that keeps us going? What is that thread that binds us on the side of the fence of non-destruction? Because somewhere in there is that indomitable will to stay non-violent that has saved us from being engulfed by violence. That's looking at the glass half full.

"*Himsa* does not need to be taught. Man as animal is violent but as spirit is non-violent. The moment he awakens to the spirit within, he cannot remain violent." The doctrine of *ahimsa* is nothing less and nothing more than a call to human beings to regard themselves as superior animals and to remind themselves of their moral and spiritual status, their dignity as human beings — as mentioned in Gandhi's concept of *Satyagraha* and his five axioms of non-violence as creed mentioned above.

At this point on the platform of non-violence, there is 'No fear'.

According to Gandhiji, "A *Satyagrahi* bids good-bye to fear. He is, therefore, never afraid of trusting the opponent.[1]

Let's reflect on Gandhiji's sentiments again as a law practitioner—"I felt it was my duty to befriend both parties and bring them together. I realized that the true function of a lawyer was to unite parties driven asunder". He shied away from violent responses and violent attacks because an eye for an eye makes the whole world blind. Having no fear in mind, one must intervene, respond with reasoning and negotiate.

Non-Violence is a potent force that must begin with the mind. We are in this new age where every moment, we witness formerly thought impossible ideas becoming possible and helping us shape our reality. There are endless discoveries in the field of science and other fields – more or less in the field of violence. So, why not give a chance to the discovery of the idea of non-violence. Non-violence is not impossible, especially when approached with 'No Fear'. Peace has no fear.

Therefore, peace must be a non-violent journey.

Notes

1. Gandhi, Arun and Sunanda with Yellin, Carol Lynn. *The Forgotten Woman: The Untold Story of Kastur, Wife of Mahatma Gandhi*. Zark Mountain Publishers, Huntsville, Arkansas, USA: 1998. p. 154.
2. Iyer, Raghavan N. *The Moral and Political thought of Mahatma Gandhi*. Oxford University Press, New Delhi, India: 2000.

9

Epilouge

(Neo-Gandhism)

> Gandhi said, "Each one has to find his peace from within. And peace, to be real, must be unaffected by outside circumstances." He said, "God needs no personal service. He serves his creatures without demanding any service for Himself in return. He is unique in this as in many other things. Therefore, servants of God are to be known by the service they render to His creatures."
>
> East and west looked at him, followed him, loved him, and yet misunderstood him.
>
> —*Herrymon Maurer*[1]

Even today while still utterly misunderstanding Gandhiji, the need for his non-violence philosophy is compelling.

"And I think, in a way, non-violence is our nature. Violence is not really our nature. If violence was our nature, we wouldn't need military academies and martial arts institutions to teach us how to kill and destroy. We ought to have been born with those instincts. But the fact that we have to learn the art of killing means that it's a learnt experience. And we can always unlearn it," said Arun Gandhi during his interview on September 11, 2006 on 'Democracy Now! The War and Peace Report' which is a daily TV/Radio news programme, hosted by Amy Goodman and Juan Gonzalez, airing on over 800 stations.

Arun Gandhi, born in South-Africa under apartheid, is the fifth grandson of Mahatma Gandhi. In 1991 he co-founded the M.K.

Gandhi Institute for Non-Violence in Memphis Tennessee, which promotes non-violence in conflict zones around the world.

September 11, 2006 has a special significance. It marks the 50th anniversary of the attacks on New York and Washington as well as it marks the 100th anniversary of the day when Mahatma Gandhi launched the modern non-violent resistance movement on September 11, 1906, called *Satyagraha* which has been adopted by many around the world to resist social injustice and oppression.

No doubt, it is on the journey of pragmatic *Satyagraha* and dynamic and active non-violence philosophy that we will unlearn our taught-violent behaviour and achieve peace. Peaceful means will give way to peaceful end.

> *Though, Peace as an end is something we hear and see all the time.*
>
> *Newsflashes are highlighted such as*
>
> *'No peace in Bo. . ..'*
>
> *'We want peace.'. .*
>
> *Television blares at us with similar news content.*
>
> *And we sit at home and wonder why there is no peace 'over there'.*

The television programmes highlight conspiracies. A majority of the shows and movies revolve around ego and vengeance and in all kinds of places starting from one's home to office and even government level. Conspiracy, ego-trip and vengeance run in a vicious never-ending spirals. This peace, that emanates from such conspiracies, ego-trips and vengeance acts, is merely a quiet moment, a silent moment, an oppressed moment in time.

Darkness does not dispel darkness, maintained Gandhiji. Therefore, it is imperative how we achieve the goal because the end defines the means. Therefore, peaceful means is the only plausible right path to achieve peace as an end, simultaneously, keeping peace dynamic and making it a way of life.

Suraj Sadan, President of The Mahatma Gandhi International Foundation (Montreal), is a visual artist who is dedicated to the promotion of the non-violent philosophy of Mahatma Gandhi through painting and drawing portraits of Gandhiji.

"Quotes of Mahatma Gandhi" is a new inspiring book by Anil Dutta Mishra, A. B. S. V. Ranga Rao, Thomas Panakal (An Indian born Montrealer Gandhian), an author of more than 200 publications) and Sohan Raj Tater.

Dr. Uma Shanker Srivastava of Montreal has dedicated his immense efforts in getting the bust of Gandhiji installed in Quebec city, (Quebec, Canada), Brossard (Quebec, Canada) and soon to be installed in Mahatma Gandhi Park in Montreal (Quebec, Canada).

The peace icon, Mahatma Gandhi, is also favourite of the recording artist Shakira. On March 19, 2010, in the official statement by her on receiving medal of honour from International Labour Organization (ILO) for her work promoting social justice recently in Geneva (Switzerland), Shakira, 33, pointed out:

> *Mahatma Gandhi said - "Be the change you want to see in the world.". . .*
>
> *"It's not too late to keep our promise to our children, but we must act now. Together, we can make education and decent work for all a reality.*[2]

According to a well known Indo-American statesman Rajan Zed, who is the chairperson of Indo-American Leadership Confederation, Mahatma Gandhi is being rediscovered in the world and many people globally revere him as one of the greatest moral, political, and peace leaders of the 20th century. Although Gandhi never set foot on America, yet he was on time magazine covers in 1930, 1931 and 1947; Time Person of the Year in 1930; and was runner up for Time Person of the Century.

Mahatma Gandhi, i.e. the great soul Gandhi, and Gandhism which is born out of South-Africa, nurtured in India and taken abroad all over the world, is still alive and flourishing today all over the globe because humans are non-violent by nature. And journey of peace is non-violent.

Peace.

Om Shanti. Om Shanti. Om Shanti.

"Non-violence in politics is a new weapon in the process of evolution. Its vast possibilities are yet unexplored."

—*Mohandas K. Gandhi*

Notes

1. Maurer, Herrymon. *Great Soul: The Growth of Gandhi*. Doubleday & Company, Inc., New York, USA: 1948. p. 100.
2. *Gandhi's words are Shakira's personal motto*. ANI, Indian Express.com. posted: Friday March 19, 2010, 10:47hrs. Nevada.

Glossary

Adharma — 'lack of dharma' in Hindi.

Adivasi — Hindi term for the indigenous people of India.

Agraha — 'to persist' in Hindi.

Ahimsa — 'non-violence' in Hindi.

Bhagwad Gita — A sacred Hindu scripture that is part of *Mahabharata* epic. It contains the philosophical dialogue of Krishna with Arjuna.

Bapu — 'father' in Hindi.

Brahmacharya — celibacy.

Charkha — spinning wheel.

Dharma — see concepts in chapter 2.

Diya — traditional Indian clay lamp lit with oil.

Emic and Etic — Emic is the point of view as a participant in a situation and Etic is the point of view of an observer from outside of the situation. These are anthropological terms.

Gita — See Bhagwad Gita.

Harijans — are untouchables. It means 'people of god' in Hindi.

Hartal — protest.

Himsa — violence.

Karmayoga — see concepts in chapter 2.

Mukti — liberation or nirvana.

Om Shanti — peace mantra.

Panchayats — a local government body at the village level in rural India.

Pandit — 'scholar' in Hindi.

Prakriti — mother nature. For details, see concepts in chapter 2.

Raj — 'rule' in Hindi

Rishis — 'sages' in Hindi.

Sabha — 'meeting' in Hindi.

Sarvodhaya — Gandhian economic model. See concepts in chapter 2.

Satya —'truth' in Hindi.

Satyagraha — 'upholding the truth'. See details in chapter 2.

Satyagrahi — a person who exercises satyagraha.

Shakti — 'power' or 'strength' in Hindi. It refers to the female power, inner strength.

Shanti — 'peace' in Hindi.

Smarpan — 'surrender' in Hindi.

Swaraj — 'self-rule' in Hindi.

Swedeshi/swadeshi — swa means 'self' or 'own' and desh means 'country'. Swadeshi refers to products made in one's country. Swadeshi movement was used as a strategy to oust the British Empire and improve India's economy.

Bibliography

Albert, Peter J. and Hoffman, Ronald. *We Shall Overcome: Martin Luther King, Jr and The Black Freedom Struggle*. Da Capo Press, USA: 1993.

Anderson, Jervis. *Bayard Rustin: Troubles I've Seen (A Biography)*. University of California Press, Berkeley and Los Angeles, California: 1998.

Attenborough, Richard. Director, *Gandhi. (movie)* 1982.

Attenborough, Richard. *(selected by) The Words of Gandhi*. New York: Newmarket Press, 1996.

Baradat, Leon P. *(4th edition) Political Ideologies: Their Origins and Impact*. Prentice Hall, Englewood Cliffs, New Jersey, USA: 1991.

Benson, Mary. (Foreword by Bishop Desmond M. Tutu) *Nelson Mandela: The Man and the Movement*. W.W. Norton & Company, New York, USA: 1986.

Bhanti, Raj. *Social Policy and Development in Rajasthan*. Himanshu Publications, Udaipur: 1995.

Bondurant, Joan Valerie. *Conquest of Violence: The Gandhian Philosophy of Conflict. (With a New Epilogue by the Author)* Princeton University Press, USA: 1958.

Borgatta, Edgar F. & Montgomery, Rhonda J. V. (Editors) *Encyclopaedia of Sociology – 2 (2nd edition)*. Macmillan Reference USA, New York: 2000.

Brown, Judith M. (editor) *Mahatma Gandhi: The Essential Writings*. Oxford University Press, Oxford, UK: 2008.

Catlin, George. *In The Path of Mahatma Gandhi*. Macdonald & Co., (Publishers) Ltd., London, England: 1948.

Clark, Robert P., *Power and Policy in The Third World.* (3rd. ed.) Macmillan, New York: 1986.

Collins, Larry and Lapierre, Dominique. *Freedom At Midnight*. Simon and Schuster, New York, USA: 1975.

Copley, Antony., *Gandhi: Against the Tide*. Oxford University Press, Oxford, UK: 1987.

Crisis inspired Many Native People, History. First Nations drum. Source: http://www.firstnationsdrum.com/fall2000/hist_oka.htm

D'Emilio, John. *lost prophet: The Life and Times of Bayard Rustin.* The University of Chicago Press, Chicago, USA: 2003.

Eliade, Mircea. *(Ed.) The Encyclopaedia of Religion.* Macmillan, New York. 1987. Vol. 11. 221-224.

Gandhi's words are Shakira's personal motto. ANI, Indian Express.com. posted: Friday March 19. 2010, 10:47hrs. Nevada.

Gandhi, Arun. *Satyagraha 100 Years Later: Gandhi Launches Modern Non-Violent Resistance Movement on Sept. 11, 1906. Talk show* on "Democracy Now! The War and Peace Report", *a daily TV/ Radio news program, hosted by Amy Goodman and Juan Gonzalez, airing on over 800 stations.* September 11, 2006.

Gandhi, Arun & Sunanda with Yellin, Carol Lynn. *The Forgotten Woman: The Untold Story of Kastur, Wife of Mahatma Gandhi.* Zark Mountain Publishers, Huntsville, Arkansas, USA: 1998.

Gandhi, M. K. (Introduction by A.P.J. Abdul Kalam) *An Autobiography or The Story of My Experiments with Truth.* Penguin Books, New Delhi, India: 2006.

Gandhi, Mahatma. *All Men Are Brothers: Autobiographical Reflections*. Continuum, New York: 1992.

Green, Martin. *Tolstoy and Gandhi, Men of Peace: A Biography*. Basic Books Inc. Publishers, New York, USA: 1983.

Gutmann, Amy. (editor) Ignatieff, Michael. *Human Rights: As Politics and Idolatry*. Princeton University Press, Princeton and Oxford: 2001.

Himelfarb, Alexander. *Dept. of Justice,* Ottawa & Richardson, C. James *Dept. of Sociology, University of New Brunswick, Sociology for Canadians: Images of Society 2nd Ed.* McGraw-Hill Rayerson Limited: 1991.

Iyer, Raghavan N., *The Moral and Political thought of Mahatma Gandhi.* Oxford University Press, New Delhi, India: 2000.

Leon P. Baradat, (4th edition) *Political Ideologies: Their Origins and Impact.* Prentice Hall, Englewood Cliffd, New Jersey: 1991.

Madan, T. N., *Images of the World: Essays on Religion, Secularism, and Culture.* Oxford University Press, New Delhi: 2006.

Maurer, Herrymon. *Great Soul: The Growth of Gandhi.* Doubleday & Company, Inc., New York, USA: 1948.

Mawdsley, Emma. "After Chipko: From Environmental to Region in Uttaranchal". *Journal of Peasant Studies.* 25 (4): 36-54. 1998.

Meer, Fatima. *Higher Than Hope: The Authorized Biography of Nelson Mandela.* Harper & Row Publishers, New York, USA: 1988.

Mishra, Anil Dutta; Rao, A.B.S.V. Ranga; Panakal, Thomas & Tater, Sohan Raj. *Quotes of Mahatma Gandhi.* Abhijeet Publications: Delhi. 2010.

Nanda, B. R., *Gandhi and his Critics.* Oxford, New Delhi: 1985.

Nehru, Jawaharlal, *Nehru and Gandhi: A selection, arranged in the order of events, from the writings and speeches of Jawaharlal Nehru.* The John Day Company: New York, USA: 1948.

Nehru, Jawaharlal. *The Discovery of India.* Oxford University Press, *Centenary edition:* January 1, 1994.

Nikhilananda, Swami. *Vivekananda: A Biography.* Calcutta, India: Advaita Ashrama, 1998.

Obomsawin, Alanis. Director, *Kanehsatake - 270 Years Of Resistance* (Oka Mohawk Uprising). *(movie)* 1993.

Panakal, Thomas. *The Journal of Gandhian Studies.* Indian Society of Gandhian Studies, New Delhi: Vol. II, No. 1 and 2, 2006.

Parks, Rosa with Gregory J. Reed. *Quiet Strength: The Faith, the Hope, and the Heart of a Woman Who Changed a Nation.* Grand Rapids, Michigan: Zondervan Publishing House, 1994.

Patel, A.R. and Khankhoje, D. P. *Rural Economics*. Sultan Chand & Sons, New Delhi: 1985.

Peaceful protest march to mark the 20th anniversary of the Oka Crisis. The Canadian Press: July 11, 2010.

Source: http://www.thewesternstar.com/Canada—World/Sports/2010-07-11/article-1532237/Peaceful-protest-march-to-mark-the-20th-anniversary-of-the-Oka-Crisis/1

Prabhu, R. K. & Rao, U. R. *(Eds)* "Between Cowardice and Violence". *The Mind of Mahatma Gandhi. (revised edition)* Ahemadabad, India: 1967.

Prabhu, R. K. & Rao, U. R. (Eds.) "The Gospel of Sarvodaya". *The Mind of Mahatma Gandhi. (revised edition)* Ahemadabad, India: 1967.

Raphael, Maryanne. *What Mother Teresa Taught Me*. St. Anthony Messenger Press, Cincinnati, Ohio: 2007.

Raphael, Maryanne & Raphael, Lennox. *Garden of Hope: Autobiography of a Marriage*. Hopewell Publications, New Jersey: 2006.

Rangan, Haripriya. *Of Myths and Monuments*. New York, Verso: 2000.

Ruskin, John. Mornings in Florence. (e-book) 1886. 182 pages.

Satyagraha, Source: www.gandhitoday.com

Selected Works of Rabindranath Tagore. Shrijee's Book International, New Delhi: 2003.

Shiva, Vandana, *Staying Alive: Women, Ecology and Development*. Kali for Women, New Delhi: 1988.

Spolia, Monika. *Exploring Gandhian Attire of Non-Violence*. Bharat Times (newspaper), Montreal: October 2007 issue. 2 & 21.

Stevenson, Leslie & Haberman, David L. (Indian Edition) *Ten Theories of Human Nature*. Oxford University Press, New York, USA: 2004.

Wikipedia, the free encyclopedia on web.

Yogananda, Paramahansa. *Autobiography of a Yogi*. Self-Realization Fellowship, USA: 2005.

Zimmerman, Larry J., *Native North America*. Little Brown and Company, Boston. 1996.

Index